W9-BMN-747

OPPORTUNITIES IN
Clinical Laboratory Science Careers

KAREN KARNI

Revised by
LUISA GERASIMO

Foreword by
Cheryl R. Caskey, M.A., C.L.S., C.L.Sp. (NCA)
President
American Society for Clinical Laboratory Science

VGM Career Books

Chicago   New York   San Francisco   Lisbon   London   Madrid   Mexico City
Milan   New Delhi   San Juan   Seoul   Singapore   Sydney   Toronto

Library of Congress Cataloging-in-Publication Data

Karni, Karen R.
    Opportunities in clinical laboratory science careers / Karen Karni ;
foreword by Cheryl Caskey—Rev. ed.
        p. cm.—(VGM opportunities series)
    Previously published as: Opportunities in medical technology
careers : clinical laboratory science.
    ISBN 0-658-01759-4 (hardcover)—ISBN 0-658-01760-8 (paperback)
    1. Medical laboratory technology—Vocational guidance. I. Karni, Karen R.
Opportunities in medical technology careers. II. Title. III. Series.

RB37.6.K47 2002
610.69'53—dc21
                                                            2001057929

VGM Career Books

A Division of The McGraw·Hill Companies

Portions of this book have been previously published in *Opportunities in
Medical Technology Careers: Clinical Laboratory Science*.

    3 4 5 6 7 8 9 0   DSH/DSH   0 1 0 9 8 7 6 5

ISBN 0-658-01759-4 (hardcover)
ISBN 0-658-01760-8 (paperback)

This book was set in Adobe Garamond by Rattray Design
Printed and bound by Lake Book Manufacturing

Cover photograph copyright © PhotoDisc

Contents

Foreword

THE PROFESSION OF clinical laboratory science continues to grow in importance, now providing approximately 70 percent of the data used for clinical decision making. It is estimated that today 400,000 to 700,000 clinical laboratory professionals work in at least 170,000 different laboratories.

The demand for clinical laboratory professionals will continue to grow as more subspecialties such as molecular diagnostics, flow cytometry, forensics, and genetic testing emerge. Physicians and other health care providers will continue to require new analyses and data to diagnose diseases and more difficult testing to monitor some disease states. The advent of wellness and preventive medicine has led to laboratory professionals being involved in consulting and screening for undetected diseases.

This book has captured the contributions and excitement of the clinical laboratory science profession through its descriptions of various clinical laboratory personnel, practice sites, typical curricula, and issues affecting clinical laboratory practice patterns. Additionally, career opportunities within and outside health care are provided. The demand for clinical laboratory professionals is predicted to grow over the next decade.

Clinical laboratory professionals are among the health professionals on the cutting edge because of the roles they play in diagnosing malignancies, detecting genetic errors, detecting inborn errors of metabolism in newborns, and identifying individuals predisposed to certain conditions such as heart disease.

As you read this book, the many opportunities in the clinical laboratory will become evident. You can work as a generalist or in different laboratory disciplines such as hematology, chemistry, microbiology, or blood bank. You can work as a consultant, inspector, manager, or educator. You can work in a variety of practice sites such as hospitals, independent labs, research labs, public health offices and labs, physician offices, or forensic laboratories as well as in industry sales and technical services. Clinical laboratory science combines science and technology in a medical career in which testing helps to diagnose, treat, and prevent diseases.

Laboratory professionals have gone on to become well-known researchers, hospital administrators, and director of the Centers for Medicare and Medicaid Services (previously known as the Health Care Finance Administration), and they have reached all levels of academia to include university president.

Career choices are often difficult. Clinical laboratory science offers a career in which you are an active and vital participant of the health care team. It will challenge and stimulate you, and you will gain much satisfaction in knowing that you make a difference in the lives of the patients you serve.

Cheryl R. Caskey, M.A., C.L.S., C.L.Sp. (NCA)
President
American Society for Clinical Laboratory Science

PREFACE

THIS BOOK PROVIDES a description of the career opportunities available to men and women within the profession of clinical laboratory science. Those interested in the biologic and chemical sciences, in performing laboratory work, in problem solving, in interacting with health care colleagues, and in serving the community and contributing to the betterment of humankind will do well to consider this profession as a career choice.

The profession of clinical laboratory science has evolved since the early 1900s. Presently there are an estimated 400,000 to 700,000 laboratory personnel in the United States, the majority being clinical laboratory scientists educated at the baccalaureate level. This book is intended to encourage students to complete this kind and level of education. Other major laboratory personnel, their job descriptions, and educational requirements are provided as well.

The terminology used in laboratory science has changed. In the past, the title "medical technologist" was used to denote a graduate of a baccalaureate program in laboratory science. Now, the title "clinical laboratory scientist" is used with increasing frequency. In this book, both titles are found. For example, the accrediting agency, the National Accrediting Agency for Clinical Laboratory Sciences (NAACLS) uses the CLS designation. The certification title "clinical laboratory scientist" is granted by the National Credentialing Agency for Laboratory Personnel. The oldest U.S. professional association of laboratory professionals, the American Society for Medical Technology, in 1993, changed its name to the American Society for Clinical Laboratory Science. The American Medical Association, through its *Allied Health Directory*, also uses the title "clinical laboratory scientist." However, the Board of Registry of the American Society of Clinical Pathologists retains the earlier designation "medical technologist" for its baccalaureate-level certified personnel.

Clinical laboratory science is supported as the preferred title because it more accurately describes this profession. However "medical technology" may still be seen. It is anticipated that students, faculty, and counselors will understand the usage of each in this book.

Everyone is ultimately confronted with the decision of selecting a career. There are those rare individuals who early in life know what they wish to do and pursue that career unwaveringly. However, most of us are not that single-minded. Indeed, this book is to help those who may be uncommitted to decide whether this profession meets their expectations, interests, and abilities.

One inevitably asks, "How can I tell if I am the kind of person who will be a successful professional in this field?" Two factors have the greatest influence upon the answer: motivation and ability. The first can be evaluated by how much an individual finds out about a profession through reading, interviews, tours, and volunteer work. The second can be evaluated by a review of a high school or college transcript. Both are crucial to the success one has in reaching a goal.

With the help of the information here, we anticipate that committed women and men will join our ranks. Clinical laboratory science offers a great diversity of job opportunities. It also provides personal satisfaction in work done meaningfully and well. Finally, it utilizes the latest advances in science and technology as new methodologies and techniques make this profession more exciting, more intricate, and more needed.

ACKNOWLEDGMENTS

THE SUCCESS OF any book is the result of collective efforts, but its shortcomings belong to the author alone. Deep appreciation is expressed to the following colleagues for their assistance: Kathleen Hansen, Britta Karlsson, Sidney Oliver, Elissa Passiment, Janice Putnam, Patricia Solberg, and Kurt Davis (Canadian Society for Medical Laboratory Science); Colonel Rodney Day (U.S. Army), Major Paula Simon (U.S. Air Force), and Captain Roy Koehn (U.S. Navy).

Also appreciated is the considerable staff assistance of Lillian Sarkinen and Claire Bjorklund.

Thanks to Michael, Erik, and Jake Karni for their patience and faith. Special thanks to Bertha and Carl Soderberg for instilling values of loyalty, commitment, and perseverance.

Leaders and staff members of the American Society for Clinical Laboratory Science have cooperated greatly in furnishing essential materials that were cited in this text and in providing general encouragement for the project.

Luisa Gerasimo wishes to thank the following professionals for their willingness to search for statistics and relevant information.

- Cheryl R. Caskey, M.A., C.L.S., C.L.Sp (NCA), President of the American Society for Clinical Laboratory Science
- Kathleen L. Hansen, President, Board of Directors, National Credentialing Agency for Laboratory Personnel (NCA); Chair, Government Affairs Committee, American Society for Clinical Laboratory Science (ASCLS); Past President ASCLS; Director, Laboratory Operations, Fairview-University Medical Center, Minneapolis
- Jeanne M. Isabel, M.S.Ed., C.L.Sp.H. (NCA), M.T. (ASCP), IAMLT Council Member, Associate Professor of Clinical Laboratory Sciences, Northern Illinois University
- Betsy Mercuri, Director of Education, Canadian Society for Medical Laboratory Science
- Patricia Solberg, Administrative Associate, University of Minnesota program in Medical Technology
- Major Martin E. Tenney, Deputy Program Manager, U.S. Army Medical Command
- Colonel Daniel R. Brown, U.S. Air Force, B.S.C, C.A.A.M.A., Director, Department of Defense Center for Laboratory Medicine
- Captain R. Gregory Craigmiles, U.S. Navy, M.S.C, Armed Forces Institute of Pathology, Office of Clinical Laboratory Affairs

Introduction

What Does a Laboratory Professional Do?

You look closely through a microscope to examine it. Stain it with different solutions. Magnify it. Whirl it. Add reagents to it. Freeze it. Separate its components. Determine its endpoints, both qualitative and quantitative. With precision. With accuracy. With speed. It takes intelligence, discipline, a positive attitude.

You need to be able to work with both your mind and your hands. To like biology and chemistry. To use exacting techniques, simple and complicated instruments, and often computers.

There are challenges: to master new principles, techniques, methodologies. To solve problems. To provide needed information. To devise new ways of testing. To perform sophisticated procedures, sometimes under pressure of time and in life or death situations.

And there is satisfaction. Demonstrating competence. Being productive in a concrete way. Providing quality service. Working with colleagues. And, most of all, knowing you have a vital part in the diagnosis, treatment, and care of your fellow human beings.

1

THE SCOPE AND PRACTICE OF CLINICAL LABORATORY SCIENCE

Overview

Clinical laboratory science, or medical technology, takes its practitioners on a fascinating journey to the very center of life, to the essence of age-old mysteries of disease and good health. Perhaps the first clinical chemistry report ever recorded was published by Sasruta, a Hindu physician writing around 600 B.C. He noted the sweet taste of diabetic urine. In ancient Greece, Hippocrates taught his students to base diagnoses on the appearance of urine. As time went on, testing became somewhat less reliant on the doctor's senses and more reliant on advances in technology. When the number of patients a doctor treated was very small, clinical testing was performed directly by the doctor. However, advances in medical knowledge, specialized technology, and testing procedures became the domain of specialists, thus freeing doctors to take the

1

time needed to treat patients. Today these specialists are known by a number of titles including laboratory technologists, clinical or medical laboratory technicians, clinical laboratory scientists, and medical technologists.

The profession is now a rapidly evolving industry of major proportions. In the United States we spend some billions of dollars each year for tests performed in more than 170,000 clinical laboratories.

Typically, through detailed microscopic, chemical, or visual analysis of specimens taken from body substances, clinical laboratory scientists identify, quantify, verify, and report the presence or absence of chemicals, microorganisms, enzymes, proteins, and other substances, and the composition and function of cells, tissues, and organs. The ten billion or more tests they perform each year help physicians screen for illnesses, diagnose diseases, determine their causes, prescribe correct treatment, prevent unwelcome drug interactions, discover substance abuse, and perhaps most important, promote good health.

Clinical laboratory scientists and other laboratory practitioners are found throughout the health care delivery system, as well as in numerous other settings. Those who work in a clinical laboratory may practice in hospitals, independent commercial laboratories, clinics, physician offices, blood banks, public health departments, ambulatory care centers, industry, and other settings. Some clinical laboratory professionals work abroad, in the Peace Corps or Project HOPE, or in private or government facilities in other countries.

Many practitioners work in clinical laboratories performing the analytical procedures just described. Many others, however, provide specialized services in a variety of essential health care roles, often in hospitals but also in other health care delivery settings. Some, for example, ensure the quality and safety of the nation's supply of blood and blood products used for transfusions in surgery, postoperatively, and for other needs. Others perform tissue and cell analyses essential for bone marrow, kidney, heart, skin, liver, and other organ transplants.

Some clinical scientists put their skills to work for *in vitro* fertilization laboratories where human sperm and ova are joined in an environment outside the living body, and then implanted (as an embryo) in a woman's uterus. Others work as researchers in public health departments where they help epidemiologists trace the origin and spread of infectious diseases. And some go on to other roles, serving as hospital infection control officers and as managers in the upper echelons of health care administration.

These are just a few of the options open to the qualified clinical laboratory professional. Consider also the array of roles outside the health care mainstream such as biogenetics; occupational health; environmental health; independent consulting; education and higher education administration; industrial research; product development, marketing, and sales; veterinary science; and forensics (criminology). Few other fields offer graduates a basic preparation for so many possible career paths.

For those students attracted to biology, chemistry, problem solving, and helping people, this profession offers many satisfying career options.

Defining the Field

Probably no other profession is both so important to health care, and yet so little known. Because clinical laboratory professionals historically have had somewhat limited contact with patients, most people know less about them than about other health care workers with whom they have contact. And yet, the information the clinical laboratory professional provides is largely responsible for the appropriateness of the care provided by physicians, pharmacists, nurses, therapists, and other health professionals. They all rely on laboratory data to make a diagnosis or implement a course of treatment that is appropriate for each patient.

Few fields in all of health care are as confusing for those outside the profession. There are many reasons for the confusion. First, clinical laboratory practitioners (the term used here for all levels of practice) are known by a bewildering number of professional titles. Second, they work in a large number and variety of settings. Third, there are differences even within the profession about what various clinical laboratory practitioners should be called, and what their roles should be.

Clinical laboratory technologists held about 350,000 to 700,000 jobs for all subsets of the field. See Table 1 for a comparison of various health care providers.

A Multifaceted Profession

To begin to understand this complex field, it helps to remember that clinical laboratory practitioners assume many roles within and outside of the health service delivery system.

It might also be helpful to remember that because the field is constantly changing (in response to new technologies, health care cost-containment pressures, variations in health care needs, and even new illnesses), new roles are being created every year.

The American Society for Clinical Laboratory Science (ASCLS), the oldest of the professional societies devoted exclusively to the profession, summarizes the scope of practice as follows in Table 1:

Table 1 Numbers of Major Health Care Providers–1999

Health Profession	Total Employed	Percentage of Total		
		Women	Black	Hispanic Origin
Registered nurses	2,128,000	92.9	9.6	3.1
Social workers	813,000	71.4	24.2	7.4
Physicians	720,000	24.5	5.7	4.8
*Laboratory personnel (est.)	449,000 to 731,000	see below	(three categories)	
Clinical laboratory technologists and technicians	338,000	78.5	19.4	5.6
*Medical scientists (total)	100,000	44.9	6.1	5.3
*Science technicians (biologic and chemical) (total)	293,000	40.8	11.0	7.3
Licensed practical nurses	357,000	95.1	18.4	5.8
Pharmacists	216,000	49.0	5.6	3.5
Dentists	173,000	16.5	1.9	3.1
Radiologic technicians	167,000	74.4	9.7	4.1
Physical therapists	144,000	73.2	5.3	5.3
Dental hygienists	106,000	99.1	2.8	1.5
Speech therapists	99,000	93.1	1.1	4.2
Dieticians	92,000	84.0	19.5	4.6
Respiratory therapists	90,000	60.6	17.6	3.3
Physicians' assistants	67,000	52.6	4.3	2.6

*Based on one-third of medical scientists and science technicians also being clinical laboratory personnel for these two categories (lower figure of estimate).
From: *Statistical Abstract of the United States*, 2000, 120th Ed. The National Data Book. Washington, D.C. pp 416-417.

The Scope of Practice of the Clinical Laboratory Sciences

The ASCLS defines the profession of clinical laboratory science as encompassing the design, performance, evaluation, reporting, interpreting, and clinical correlation of clinical laboratory testing and the management of all aspects of these services. Clinical laboratory tests are utilized for the purpose of diagnosis, treatment monitoring, and prevention of disease. The profession includes generalists as well as individuals qualified in a number of specialized areas of expertise, including microbiology/virology, hematology, immunology, transfusion medicine, clinical chemistry, endocrinology, toxicology, cytogenetics, and molecular diagnostics. Integral features of each of the specialties may include research, consultation, education, information management, marketing, and administration. The profession has a code of ethics that sets forth the principles and standards by which clinical laboratory professionals practice.

Description of Scope of Practice

Clinical laboratory personnel, as members of the health care delivery team, are responsible for ensuring reliable and accurate laboratory test results that contribute to the diagnosis, treatment, prognosis, and prevention of physiological and pathological conditions in humans.

The hallmarks of quality clinical laboratory testing are: performing the correct test, on the right person, at the right time, producing accurate test results, with the best outcome, in the most cost-effective manner. This is accomplished by:

A. Assessing, designing, evaluating, and implementing new laboratory test methods.

B. Evaluating the appropriateness of existing and new laboratory methods for clinical utility, cost-effectiveness, and cost-benefit analysis.

C. Developing, implementing, and reporting results of clinical laboratory services research (i.e., within the context of cost, quality, and access).

D. Designing and implementing cost-effective delivery models for clinical laboratories, including their services and personnel.

E. Developing and implementing a comprehensive Quality Management System to include:
  1. quality control and assurance of clinical laboratory testing services;
  2. competency assessment of personnel;
  3. integration with other aspects of the health care delivery system for ensuring appropriate utilization of clinical laboratory testing services;
  4. continuous process improvement activities to maximize human resources.
F. Designing, implementing, and evaluating process for the education of new clinical laboratory personnel, and the continued education, development, and career growth of clinical laboratory professionals.
G. Promoting awareness and understanding of the use of clinical laboratory testing services to the health care consumer, physician, other health care personnel, health care administrators, and policy makers.

(*Source:* "Scope of Practice Position Paper." Approved August 2, 2001, by the American Society for Clinical Laboratory Science House of Delegates.)

Although many definitions exist, in the simplest terms, this profession is concerned with providing information based on the performance of analytical tests upon body substances to detect evidence of or to prevent disease or impairment, and to promote and monitor good health.

Among the thousands of routine and complex tests available are those well known to most people. Almost everyone has had at least one complete blood count (CBC performed to detect blood disorders such as anemia or leukemia, or a urinalysis used to screen for kidney or other conditions. Most of us have had our blood typed and tested for compatibility, so that when we donate or receive blood, we and others are ensured of a safe, effective transfusion. More and more of us are having cholesterol levels checked, to lessen the risk of heart disease. Some monitor their own blood sugar levels to correct conditions like diabetes. Other well-known clinical laboratory tests include antibody tests for viral or immunological diseases, throat or blood cultures for microbiologic infections, tests for alcohol or drug levels, and coagulation tests for clotting disorders.

Since its origins, the field of clinical laboratory science has grown in complexity and responsibility from a helping occupation limited to elementary functions, to its status today as a multifaceted profession that includes many other roles as well.

A current definition, then, might read as follows:

Clinical laboratory professionals assume many roles within and outside health services delivery. In traditional laboratory services they provide essential clinical information based on performing and ensuring the quality of tests of human body tissues, blood, fluids, and other substances. Integral parts of their responsibility are verifying, interpreting, and reporting the results of these tests to attending physicians. Many laboratory practitioners assist physicians in correlating test results with patient data and recommend tests and test sequences in light of known clinical considerations. They also perform a wide range of management and supervisory roles, including serving as clinical laboratory directors, managers of laboratory sections, and supervisors of other technologists, technicians, and phlebotomists.

Laboratory professionals are expected to contribute to the body of knowledge comprising the profession. Their services are essential for preventing, detecting, and diagnosing disease and impairment, and for promoting good health.

Clinical laboratory scientists may also choose among many other roles within the health service delivery system but outside the traditional laboratory, including critical research roles; health care management and administration roles; independent consulting; and positions in infection control, public health, and epidemiology, to name a few.

Those who do not choose careers in health care may choose among education and higher education administration; diagnostic equipment, pharmaceutical, and other types of industrial research and product development, marketing, sales, or product representation; veterinary science; forensics; environmental or occupational safety and health; and other career paths.

Changes in the Field

Few fields are undergoing change so quickly as clinical laboratory science. A definition showing the scope of this profession and hinting at this change was offered in *Shaping the Future of Clinical Laboratory Practice: Proceedings of the Conference* over a decade ago:

> The laboratory profession does not refer to the hospital alone. Even within the hospital it does not refer to the physical space that the laboratory occupies. The laboratory profession encompasses those activities of performing, reporting, interpreting and correlating laboratory tests designed for the promotion of health [and the] prevention and treatment of disease through the application of scientific principles of biology, chemistry, and physics as they relate to [human] physiologic and biochemical processes. The laboratory profession includes a number of defined, specialized areas of competence and also incorporates social science to serve its primary purpose. Further, research, consultation, education and administration are integral features of the profession.

This comment that the profession is not bound by the four walls of the laboratory is very important. The reference, of course, is to the very rapid changes the profession is experiencing, even now, as a consequence of new developments in technology and health care economics.

Several technological developments have changed the profession radically. First, refinements in computers have made it possible to process, transfer, and store huge amounts of information. Second, the perfection of dry reagents used in clinical analysis have extended the shelf life of these chemicals, improved their portability, and made them easier to use. Third, the discovery of the monoclonal antibody has allowed clinical laboratory scientists to detect even minute quantities of a specific substance contained in a body specimen. Fourth, new laboratory subspecialty areas have emerged. Some examples follow: Molecular diagnostics involves the use, for example, of the polymerase chain reaction (PCR) to identify small regions of nucleic acids in diseases such as cystic fibrosis or Huntington's disease. Flow cytometry utilizes differences in density gradients and monoclonal antibodies to distinguish mononuclear cells, thus aiding in the diagnosis of various leukemias or lymphomas. Cytogenetics uses the analysis of chromosome number and structure to diagnose diseases such as Down's syndrome, Klinefelter's syndrome, or Turner's syndrome. The mapping of the Human Genome Project has been a huge effort to unravel the mysteries of human genetics. Completed in June 2001, it has already begun to change the ways genetic illnesses are diagnosed and treated. Electron microscopy involves the magnification of cells 100,000 times to study their ultrastructure—whether normal, inflammatory, or neoplastic (cancerous). All of these new specialty areas utilize advanced scientific biotechnology, and they may require advanced (often on-the-job and post-baccalaureate degree) training. These new areas also enhance employment possibilities.

Some of these advances have propelled the manufacture of small desk-top testing instruments and even smaller test kits, such as those used in pregnancy testing. In turn, these instruments and kits have made it possible to perform some common tests in doctors' offices and ambulatory care centers, at hospital stations, and even at home, rather than in traditional laboratory settings.

New test kits, new procedures, new instruments (some large, some small), and other technological advancements are changing the nature and expanding the boundaries of traditional laboratory practice. They are sparking new ideas among educators and managers about the roles the profession should and must take on in tomorrow's laboratory, with and without walls. It may be early to say exactly what effects those changes will have on test menus, employment patterns, and health services delivery. But change always brings opportunity, and the profession is already anticipating what new opportunities the future holds.

Principal Practice Areas Within the Field

The following major practice areas within the field are adapted from brief descriptions provided in *Medical Technology Program*, a pamphlet prepared by the Medical Technology Program of the Michigan State University, East Lansing, Michigan:

Clinical Chemistry: Analysis of bodily fluids for chemical constituents including glucose, protein, cholesterol, and electrolytes to detect diseases such as diabetes, heart attacks, or kidney failure.

Hematology: Evaluation of red blood cells, white blood cells, and platelets for diseases like anemia and leukemia.

Hemostasis: Evaluation of blood clotting to detect diseases like hemophilia or disseminated intravascular coagulation (DIC).

Microbiology: Identification of bacteria, viruses, fungi, and parasites that cause infections, as well as of the antibiotics that may be effective in treatment.

Urinalysis: Physical, chemical, and microscopic analysis of urine, which can indicate disease within the urinary tract or other body systems.

Immunohematology: Blood typing, antibody screening and identification, and other tests to provide safe and compatible blood for transfusion; also called blood banking.

Immunology: Evaluation of the body's immune system to detect diseases of impaired immune function and to ensure the compatibility of tissues and organs for transplantation.

Job Outlook

According to the 2000–2001 *Occupational Outlook Handbook*, there were 313,000 clinical laboratory technologists and technicians in 1998. Employment of clinical laboratory workers is expected to grow as fast as the average for all occupations through the year 2008. The volume of laboratory tests will continue to grow with the increase in population and the development of new types of tests. On the other hand, many employers such as hospitals and independent laboratories have recently undergone consolidation and restructuring. These changes have increased productivity and allowed the same number of personnel to perform a greater number of tests.

There is a strong need for new people to enter the field because many openings will be created as current workers transfer to related fields, retire, or stop working for some other reason. In fact in June 2000 almost twenty groups (most of which were professional laboratory science societies) came together at a meeting entitled "Summit on the Shortage of Clinical Laboratory Personnel." The summary of the meeting leaves no doubt that the baby boom generation is entering retirement age and that the people inside the field—those who are actually responsible for staffing labs—see a serious need for new professionals. These societies are working together to find ways to attract bright and talented people to the field.

Currently there are many cities and rural areas in the United States reporting shortages of clinical laboratory personnel. Pockets with a strong need for staff offer attractive starting salary and benefit packages for those willing to relocate. The American Hospital Association reported a shortage of laboratory technologists in June 2001, listing a hospital vacancy rate of 12 percent. The journal *Clinical Laboratory Science* led its 2001 summer edition with an article about shortages in laboratory personnel. The American Association of Clinical Pathologists offers reprints from a fifteen-page scholarly article detailing shortages in laboratory personnel and associated increases in salaries on its website.

Clearly there is a great need for qualified people to enter this field in the coming years. Since the need for workers in any industry can fluctuate, a visit to industry Web pages will be helpful in gaining an up-to-date understanding of the market in your area. Local librarians are often excellent at helping find sources of current information on areas of interest to their patrons.

Factors Affecting Allied Health Employment Predictions

Allied health professionals comprise more than one hundred occupations other than medicine, dentistry, pharmacy, and nursing, and they are not always direct care givers. Employment outlooks for most allied health fields, including clinical laboratory science, vary from forecaster to forecaster. This is partly due to radical changes in health care economics initiated in the 1980s and thereafter. For example, in 1983 the government implemented the Prospective Payment System (PPS), which essentially paid for much of the care of Medicare patients according to their diagnosis, not by numbers of tests needed or diagnostic procedures performed. This practice was intended to reduce laboratory and X-ray utilization, since hospitals would lose money if excessive testing was performed. The effects of the PPS on laboratory testing were not as profound as in the mergers and closures that occurred in some institutions. Many hospitals merged into "health care systems" to reduce costs and attract patients. Others were left to fend for themselves and some—especially in inner cities or in rural areas—could not survive, and closed.

In 1988 the federal government also enacted "CLIA-88," the Clinical Laboratory Improvement Act of 1988. Its intent and emphasis was to regulate all laboratories—whether in small physician offices or in academic medical centers. By 2001 more than 170,000 laboratories were identified and ensuing regulation was attempted using "test complexity," i.e. laboratories performing very simple tests could be registered but not inspected. Those laboratories performing highly complex testing, however, were to engage in proficiency testing and expect on-site inspections.

In addition in the early 1990s "managed care" became a profound movement in the United States. This involved the growth and expansion of health maintenance organizations (HMOs). (An HMO is a prepaid and organized health care system that serves a defined population. The enrolled population enters into a contract with the organization, agreeing to pay, or have paid on their behalf, a fixed sum, in return for which the HMO makes available the health care personnel, facilities, and services that the population may require.)

Persons enrolled in managed care tend to have fewer tests performed. As a result laboratory personnel needed to staff HMO laboratories are thought to be fewer in number. HMO laboratories may be organized differently from hospital laboratories. Many have satellite laboratories for routine and simple tests, and a central laboratory where complex, unusual, or difficult tests are performed. The satellite laboratories may be staffed by lesser trained personnel; the central, by baccalaureate-level practitioners.

Then in the 1990s the federal government initiated strong measures to contain and reduce health care costs, which in 2000 exceeded $1.2 trillion, or 14 percent of the gross domestic product. Both the Democrats and Republicans brought forth health care plans intended to cut Medicare reimbursements for physicians, hospitals, outpatient settings, clinics, ambulatory care settings, and laboratories. Their efforts were to reduce reimbursement to clinical laboratories. As reimbursement decreased, some laboratories reorganized and downsized, resulting in fewer personnel being employed.

Another problem is seen in the slim amount of data available about the allied health professions as compared with the wealth of information concerning medicine. Lesser public interest in the allied health professions may be due partly to the fact that women predominate in many of them. Others note that many of these fields, like laboratory science, are difficult to define. They point to the numerous, often overlapping titles, and to the fact that some health fields, including laboratory science, are not uniformly licensed and thus lack the usual "scope of practice" definitions found in licensure laws for fields like nursing, pharmacy, or medicine.

One thing that seems certain—whether ill or healthy, people will always require medical information. Technological changes create new opportunities. Changes in the way we travel and do business globally mean that humans are exposed to an ever-widening array of diseases. Global climate change even gets into the act: In North America, as average temperatures have increased, insect-borne illnesses, such as malaria, that were once thought of as equatorial illnesses, are now being discovered and treated in northern cities across the United States. Clinical laboratory personnel will always be needed to help create, perform, and interpret the tests that help physicians care for people.

Most national organizations representing laboratory practitioners remain optimistic about employment. These organizations collect information about their personnel and monitor changes the profession is experiencing. Because they are closer than other observers to the day-to-day realities of practice, and because they have so much at stake when occupational forecasts are mistaken, they often detect important demographic currents earlier and more accurately.

Supply Factors

The supply of qualified personnel has a great deal to do with whether job outlooks are vigorous or not. When supply does not keep up with demand, the employment outlook, of course, favors the job seeker.

Investigations conducted by the American Society for Medical Technology (ASMT—now the American Society for Clinical Laboratory Science, ASCLS) and by the American Society of Clinical Pathologists (ASCP) and its Board of Registry suggest that the shortages of clinical laboratory science practitioners are increasing.

The American Society of Clinical Pathologists has reported vacancies as well. These are seen in Table 2.

Although the predicted shortage in new laboratory personnel hasn't become quite as serious as expected, many inside the field still worry there could be a shortage of clinical laboratory workers. There are several reasons for the concern, and they include some simple demographic facts. The generation sometimes referred to as "Generation X" that follows the "baby boomers" (those born between 1946 and 1964) is smaller and thus there is increased competition across all professions for the smaller number of high school and college graduates. Women who might have been drawn

Table 2 ASCP Board of Registry Survey Results Vacancy Rate in 1996, 1998, and 2000 Mean Percent (%)

	1996	*1998*	*2000*
Medical Technologist/CLS Staff	8.2	10.2	11.1
Medical Technologist/CLS Supervisor	8.6	9.3	12.5
Medical Technologist Manager	7.7	15.4	13.3
Cytotechnologist Staff	7.1	10.5	20.6
Cytotechnologist Supervisor	12.5	10.0	10.0
Histologic Technician	13.0	12.9	16.1
Histotechnologist	5.3	10.3	22.3
Histologic Supervisor	10.0	20.0	20.0
Medical Laboratory Technician	9.4	11.1	14.3
Phlebotomist	12.5	12.3	18.1

From: *Cactus Chronicle*. Newsletter of the Arizona Society for Clinical Laboratory Science. 24:3, 2001.

to an allied health field now have more choice in career area and are increasingly choosing careers not traditionally seen as female. Witness the fact that many medical schools are reporting that their class numbers are more than half female. In addition, salary "compression" in allied health fields may make other careers more attractive to those of either sex.

Supply of future workers is affected by what people observe in the news and in their own lives. Many clinical laboratory professionals point to the fact that laboratory workers are less visible than people working in nursing or other fields of health care. News stories can create unrealistic fears that might keep students from wanting laboratory work. Although labs are safer now than ever, some people may hear stories of AIDS or hepatitis and fear risk of exposure to these or other diseases. The risk of accidental exposure in the rigorously controlled laboratory setting is truly miniscule, but that may not be known among students considering their long-term career options.

These developments may be expected to continue to influence the supply pool of future allied health practitioners, including those in clinical laboratory science. To the extent that demand and supply influence how the marketplace sets compensation packages (salaries and benefits), and to the extent that current conditions prevail, these factors are expected to increase the likelihood of a favorable employment outlook for clinical laboratory science graduates.

Demand

Major factors affecting demand for medical technological services of course also escalate demand for qualified practitioners. These include general population demographics, technological developments, and social developments. Even the effect of climate change on infectious diseases will increase the need for testing. According to the Bureau of Labor Statistics:

> [c]ontinued expansion of the clinical laboratory field is foreseen for three fundamental reasons. First is the increase in disease and disability that will accompany rapid growth of the middle-aged and older population. Second is the probability of new, more powerful diagnostic tests. Advances in biotechnology have already changed testing methods through the use of monoclonal antibodies and other advanced technologies that permit rapid, simple and accurate testing. As further advances occur, they are likely to spur more testing. And lastly, research laboratories that work to find the cause, treatment and cure for diseases such as acquired immune deficiency syndrome (AIDS) are expanding dramatically in response to increased funding from public and private sources.

The size and composition of the population as a whole has a major effect on demand for health care, and thus the potential to affect the employment outlook significantly. As the baby boom generation ages there is a corresponding increase in demand for and intensity of consumption of health care resources.

Other population factors will have an as yet uncertain effect on demand. For instance, the proportion of minorities in the U.S. population will increase by the year 2008. Factors such as diminished financial and geographic access to health care among minorities will have an impact on demand; the higher prevalence among some minorities of chronic diseases (such as diabetes, cancer, and heart disease) also will affect demand.

Technological change—driven by advances discussed earlier and soft technologies such as genetic engineering—is revolutionizing clinical laboratory science. One prediction states:

Implanted biosensors will give "real-time" health status reports and diminish the lag in results for many tests. Nuclear magnetic resonance will help identify the chemical makeup of tissues; DNA probes and molecular biology will transform how and when diseases and organisms are identified; robots will handle biohazardous materials and repetitive work alike; bar codes will simplify specimen handling from the bedside throughout the laboratory.

(Pill-sized sensors are already being used to help diagnose illness. Tiny cameras report images to computer enhanced graphics screens allowing doctors to "see" inside without resorting to surgery.)

These and other expected advancements not only will expand the variety of tests available, but probably will also increase the number of tests performed. Technology will have different effects on demand for practitioners at different levels. But if history is any guide, as many jobs will be created as will be taken away by automation.

Social developments also have increased demand and, interacting with new technologies, will continue to do so. For instance, changes in attitudes toward drugs and other substances, combined with technological advancements, have helped turn testing for drug use from a relatively minor field into a multimillion dollar industry. More growth is anticipated as legal and ethical questions are resolved. Similarly, the identification of human immunodeficiency virus (HIV) coupled with medical, epidemiological, legal, political, ethical, and other evaluations of its priority, have made the phrase "AIDS diagnostic tests" a household expression. Thanks to advancements in biogenetics and bioengineering, other developments like these will occur with increased demand for laboratory services and qualified practitioners.

Outlook for Technologists (Scientists) and Technicians

Clinical laboratory scientists usually hold a bachelor's degree or above, while technicians are likely to have attended a technical school or community college. Regarding employment outlooks for laboratory personnel, the Bureau of Labor Statistics notes:

> Employers' preferences vary so much that it is hard to generalize about future prospects for the different levels of clinical laboratory personnel. On the one hand, demand for technologists is likely to be sustained by the complexity of much clinical testing; the need for in-depth knowledge and independent judgment to verify test results and advise physicians; expansion of research laboratory facilities; and technologists' greater versatility. . . . On the other hand, advances in laboratory automation will continue to routinize certain tests, which may be favorable for technicians. . . . Like other areas of health care, the clinical laboratory is undergoing change on a scale that makes it extremely difficult to project future trends. For both technologists and technicians, demand will vary among employment settings, and job prospects will be affected by diverse factors including economic conditions; structure of the clinical laboratory market; strategies by health care providers seeking to enter the market; third-party reimbursement policy and other profit considerations; and changes in laboratory [personnel] licensure and staffing regulations.

Most experts within the profession would agree that caution is warranted in predicting how key questions will affect the outlook for the practitioner levels of scientist and technician. Managers will always have to weigh the pros and cons of hiring a clinical laboratory scientist versus a technician. Many jobs require the versatility, productivity, and judgment of a person with a college degree. However, these skills come with a higher salary. Technological changes will clearly affect the need for workers of all types in the industry. New laws and regulations also can affect demand for clinical laboratory scientists or technicians. And finally, there is the question of the ever increasing number of user friendly tests. Will these tests mean changes in the way laboratories around the country work?

Salaries Outlook

Results of several recent studies show that salaries and benefits are rising across all categories and levels of laboratory practice. In some areas, employers are offering tuition payments, relocation expenses, and one-time, lump-sum payments for initial employment. In fact, working teams composed of all the major professional groups meeting at the "Summit on the Shortage of Clinical Laboratory Personnel" suggested that the societies themselves could improve recruitment of students. Suggestions included: offering educational outreach and mentoring programs to less-well-served areas like inner cities and rural schools, special loan programs, and opportunities for work in laboratories while still in school.

The Bureau of Labor Statistics, which is an arm of the U.S. Department of Labor, projects a 10 to 20 percent increase in the employment of clinical laboratory scientists and technicians through the year 2008. Some journals such as the *Jobs Rated Almanac* give clinical laboratory science an even higher projected growth rate. The American Society for Clinical Laboratory Science gives starting salaries ranging from $30,000 up to $50,000 annually. The range reflects the difference factors like geographic location will make on how much a new person can expect to earn.

Because employers have to compete for applicants in some areas, those searching for jobs in areas currently experiencing a shortage can demand and receive much higher starting salaries. Of course, educational level impacts starting salaries as well. Table 3 can help clarify some of the career levels possible to attain, based on years and type of education.

Most profession leaders predict rising salaries and an increased demand for services. (Currently most laboratory workers are not unionized.)

Recalling that 75 percent of laboratory personnel are female, experts predict that the number of women in the labor force will increase more than the number of men—already women constitute half of the workforce. As a result the U.S. economy will be more dependent on college-educated women than at any time in

Table 3 Median Pay Rates (Dollars per Hour) in 1996, 1998, and 2000

	1996	*1998*	*2000*
Medical Technologist/CLS Staff	15.4	16.0	17.9
Medical Technologist/CLS Supervisor	18.6	19.8	21.5
Medical Technologist Manager	22.0	24.3	27.0
Cytotechnologist Staff	18.0	19.0	21.3
Cytotechnologist Supervisor	21.9	23.1	25.9
Histologic Technician	13.5	13.5	15.3
Histotechnologist	15.0	15.6	18.0
Histologic Supervisor	17.9	18.8	21.0
Medical Laboratory Technician	12.0	12.9	14.0
Phlebotomist	8.5	9.0	9.9

Note: To convert to annual wages, multiply the hourly pay rate by 2080 (52 weeks x 40 hours/week).

From: *Cactus Chronicle*. Newletter of the Arizona Society for Clinical Laboratory Science. 24:3, 2001.

the past. Science-based technical fields especially will be more competitive with each other for fewer qualified graduates. That will increase pressures on traditionally female, science-based fields like clinical laboratory science and other allied health professions to make their salaries more attractive.

Even in the best of times, salary levels vary from locale to locale, and even from employer to employer according to regional supply and demand and underlying economic forces. Therefore, the figures included here should be taken only as broad indications of salary levels as presented in the early part of the twenty-first century.

Job Satisfaction

Clinical laboratory science is an extremely rewarding profession for bright, science-oriented individuals who wish to apply a rich, broad-based body of scientific knowledge to health care. Built on a curriculum similar to premedicine or prepharmacy, this field integrates several bioscience disciplines as well as physiology, pathology, and increasingly, computer and management sciences. These factors make a degree in this field an excellent springboard for many career options.

Historically, clinical laboratory professionals have looked to themselves for knowledge of a job well done. Few people within, and fewer outside, the health care system understand their demanding roles in the "control room" of health services delivery. Even those many patients whose lives have been saved by a laboratory professional are unlikely to understand the role that the laboratory has played in their care and recovery.

Public awareness of the field is increasing, however. The technological abilities that have made testing for substance abuse a multimillion dollar industry, and the AIDS tragedy, symbolically have brought the laboratory from the depths of the hospital to the public's living room. Errors in Pap screening that brought about some women's deaths have made front-page news. Today most people understand the risks to themselves of a positive blood alcohol or cocaine test, or the implications of a positive HIV test.

The public has come to better realize what laboratorians have done to ensure the safety of the nation's blood supply. That public has also realized the importance of proper tissue "matching"—performed by laboratory technologists—in tissue and organ transplants (e.g., a blood group A heart cannot be transplanted into a blood group O recipient). It has also become more aware of what laboratory professionals can reveal in genetic diseases (e.g., Down's syndrome), biochemical diseases (e.g., phenylketonuria), or age-associated diseases (e.g., heart attacks in persons with high cholesterol and high LDL—low density lipoprotein—levels).

The international concern over "Mad Cow Disease" (bovine spongiform encephalopathy, or BSE) in the 1980s, and the subsequent collapse of the beef markets in many parts of the world, brought new attention to veterinary testing for animal disease. In 1996 British health officials identified a similar disease in humans and suddenly the world started paying very close attention. The disease was named variant Creutzfeldt-Jacob Disease (vCJD). Eating cattle carrying BSE can lead to vCJD in humans. A very slow moving but lethal disease, vCJD can take from five to ten or even more years to emerge.

At the time of this writing, more than one hundred people in Europe have died from vCJD, and because of the mysterious nature of the disease, it is impossible to clearly predict how many new victims will be claimed. Because this disease, and many others like it, is essentially proteins called *prions* gone awry, there is currently no test for it. Professional laboratory scientists are working very hard to develop a way to test for this serious disease and its variants in animals and humans around the world. This is just one of many veterinary science issues that directly impact food safety and thus human economic and physical health.

Increasingly, thanks to these examples, the public is learning to appreciate the laboratory professional's knowledge, skills, and dedication. Clinical laboratory science is an exacting, precise profession. It rewards the abilities of the competent practitioner with the knowledge that his or her skills and persistence have saved lives, cracked a stubborn diagnostic puzzle, prevented a lethal transfusion, or discovered the problem whose solution starts the patient on the road to recovery.

The practice of clinical laboratory science brings unique satisfactions. Clinical laboratory scientists are health care investigators who journey to the center of life and see its many mysteries up close. Those who work in large medical center and research laboratories are responsible for utilizing millions of dollars worth of state-of-the-art technology and have the opportunity to work with procedures, techniques, and tools at the forefront of basic and clinical research. This is due to the increasing applicability of advances in molecular biology, electronics, laser technologies, biosensors, and other fields that make the clinical laboratory one of the first arenas for new "soft" and "hard" technologies.

Wherever they work, the skills of laboratory practitioners are required in situations ranging from the long-term discovery of a new test to diagnose a certain disease, to the fast-paced, life-and-death intensity of the emergency room and operating theater. Laboratorians are among the few health care professionals to witness and experience the challenge of the entire range of human disorders, as well as the joys of the full health potential of humans.

Medical diagnosis and good health care depend on the clinical laboratory professional's skills, knowledge, judgment, and integrity. Because it is essential to the mission of the physician, nurse, pharmacist, physical or respiratory therapist, or other member of the health care team, laboratory science can be an extremely demanding field. Much of the laboratory practitioner's work must be done quickly, and *all* of it must be accurate. There is no margin for error because mistakes in the laboratory may mean inappropriate medical care, an ensuing serious or debilitating condition, and even death.

Like any other, this profession has some less attractive aspects that have to be balanced with its advantages. Within clinical practice, opportunities for advancement are somewhat modest; as in any hierarchy, there are fewer senior- than entry-level positions. Also, although the rich diversity in the profession's knowledge base permits numerous career paths, there may be employment limitations if one wishes to, for example, practice in a certain sought-out geographic area, work days only, or take ten years off to raise a family.

Stress, too, is an occupational hazard for professionals in clinical practice. Demands for accurate and timely results come not only from attending physicians and nurses, but also from managers oriented to the bottom line who stress that "time is money."

Image is an issue. Because the public is less aware of this profession than of other health care fields, laboratory practitioners get less credit than they deserve. (Who sends flowers to the immunohematology professional providing safe and compatible blood for a newborn during an exchange transfusion?)

Finally, although salaries are rising, and while benefits and other incentives are also improving, many practitioners believe that clinical laboratory salaries lag somewhat behind those of other health care professions such as physical therapists. Reasons often cited include the profession's low public profile; carryover practices permitting entrance into the field via nontraditional routes, such as on-the-job training; blurred job descriptions; and intraprofessional disagreements about personnel standards and job descriptions that ultimately make negotiations with health care administrators and other employers difficult.

Certainly one factor not unique to clinical laboratory science is that the majority of its practitioners are women. According to the Institute of Medicine's *Allied Health Services: Avoiding Crises*, "compensation for the allied health professions should be understood in the context of women's earnings, because women (predominate in) many allied health fields. Occupations in which women represent the majority of workers tend to rank lower in terms of earnings than male dominated occupations." However, recent studies show that the gender gap in earnings is steadily closing.

Although almost everywhere, experts agree, starting salaries are reasonably strong, the Institute of Medicine (IOM) further claims that "(i)ncreases in earnings over the length of a career are substantially lower in allied health fields than in (selected) other occupations." This "salary compression" is among the issues that employers must address for all allied health professions and for nursing and laboratory science in particular, in order to attract new recruits and prevent experienced and competent professionals from leaving the field.

Summary

Clinical laboratory science represents exciting opportunities for individuals who are interested in science, technology, and helping humankind. Those in the field who enjoy their work state these reasons for job satisfaction:

- pride in the profession and what it brings to health care
- sense of accomplishment in work that is done well
- the nature of the work: challenging, interesting, requiring reasoning and excellent judgment
- use of cutting-edge biotechnologies
- use of problem-solving abilities
- a team effort and esprit de corps among coworkers
- interaction with other health providers
- recognition for being a professional
- a sense of being essential in the detection, diagnosis, monitoring, and cure of disease
- a sense of independence, with little supervision needed
- good and varied employment opportunities following graduation and thereafter

2

Work Sites

Clinical laboratory practitioners today are found in many settings—almost everywhere professional health services are provided. Opportunities exist here and abroad and in traditional (e.g., hospital) and nontraditional settings, such as the Peace Corps or emergency care facilities.

That was not always the case. In earlier days, the laboratory professional worked exclusively in a hospital-based laboratory as an aide to a physician called a pathologist, who is a specialist in medicine concerned with the study of disease, its causes, and its consequences.

Today, thanks to rapid advances in testing technology and the need for laboratory services, laboratories are no longer confined to hospitals, and laboratory professionals fulfill *much* broader responsibilities.

Laboratory Distribution

Most laboratory tests are performed in one of three categories: hospital laboratories, independent laboratories (e.g., referral laboratories), and laboratories in physician offices. (See Table 4.)

Most laboratories are found in physician offices. In fact more than half of all U.S. clinical laboratories are found in these settings. Hospital laboratories (8,518) make up only 5 percent of all laboratories, yet they perform the greatest percentage of tests.

Hospitals and laboratories offer a large number and variety of tests. They also hire and continue to employ individuals educated as laboratorians. For complex testing, these institutions tend to hire greater numbers of baccalaureate-level personnel. They have also been highly regulated since 1966.

In HMOs and clinics with simple, standardized testing and a relatively healthy clientele, two-year technicians may predominate, under the supervision of a laboratory technologist. What then are the usual work settings for laboratory personnel? Brief descriptions follow.

Table 4 Kinds of Clinical Laboratories in the U.S. (Registered by CLIA*)

Institution	Numbers
Hospitals	8,518
Home Health Agency	7,313
Community Clinic	5,983
Skilled Nursing Facility	14,670
Physician Office	96,896
Others**	37,616
Total	170,996

*CLIA is a government agency that regulates many laboratories. (From: Clinical Laboratory Improvement Act, 1988.)
**Includes laboratories such as those in ambulatory surgical centers, blood banks, independent laboratories, renal disease dialysis facilities, and others.

Source: CLIA website, April 2001 data.

Laboratory Settings

Small Hospitals

Most clinical laboratories, such as those in hospitals, are organized into sections by the type of work performed there. In small hospitals, those with fewer than one hundred beds, the laboratory may be divided into the following four areas (see Chapter 1 for a more detailed explanation of these laboratory areas):

- chemistry and urinalysis
- hematology and coagulation
- microbiology including bacteriology, parasitology, and mycology
- blood banking and serology (also called immunology)

In a small hospital, all laboratory sections would most likely be in one large room, with specific areas delineated for each kind of analysis, for example, chemistry or hematology. In the small hospital, laboratory staff would probably include a baccalaureate-level laboratory administrator who also performs procedures, one other baccalaureate technologist, three laboratory technicians, and a part-time secretary. All laboratory personnel would be expected to perform all tests, work evenings and weekends, and take "call" on a rotational basis.

Medium Hospitals

In a medium-sized hospital, one hundred to four hundred beds, the laboratory most likely would be divided into sections discrete from one another. Typical staff size will vary based on the patient clientele and mission of the hospital (see Table 5).

Table 5 Various Laboratory Settings and Numbers/Kinds of Personnel Employed

Suburban hospital
150 beds

- 19 technologists
- 4 medical laboratory technicians
- 1 phlebotomist
- 3 clerks
- 27 Total

Independent (commercial) laboratory

- 19 technologists
- 10 medical laboratory technicians
- 6 cytotechnologists
- 12 specimen processors
- 12 phlebotomists
- 6 client clerks
- 5 lab assistants
- 10 couriers (drivers)
- 80 Total

Children's acute care hospital
150 beds

- 34 technologists
- 11 medical laboratory technicians
- 2 histologic technicians
- 12 phlebotomists, EKG technicians, and others
- 59 Total

Acute care county hospital
450 beds

- 82 technologists
- 19 laboratory technicians
- 2 cytotechnologists
- 3 histologic technicians
- 7 phlebotomists
- 113 Total

University (tertiary care hospital; includes the teaching and research mission of a university hospital)
580 beds

- 307 technologists
- 31 medical laboratory technicians
- 3 cytotechnologists
- 5 histologic technicians
- 6 scientists (Ph.D. level)
- 6 phlebotomists
- 2 autopsy technicians
- 3 EKG technicians
- 5 computer operators
- 368 Total

Health maintenance organization
20 clinic sites

- 16 technologists
- 112 medical laboratory technicians
- 2 lab aids
- 6 phlebotomists
- 136 Total

Regional blood bank

- 33 technologists
- 17 medical laboratory technicians
- 5 clerks
- 55 total

For example, a suburban hospital of 150 beds would be expected to have laboratory tests performed for residents in that geographic area in need of diagnosis, surgery, or rehabilitation. Thus a 150-bed suburban general care hospital may employ only twenty-seven persons in the laboratory. In contrast, an acute care pediatrics hospital of the same size would employ considerably more laboratory personnel. This hospital requires a larger staff due to the intensity of care and laboratory data needed for very ill infants and children.

Large Hospitals

In a large hospital, one would expect many specialty and subspecialty areas. For example, the chemistry unit might include drug analysis, enzymology, endocrinology, electrolytes, a "stat" (emergency) lab, and urinalysis. Laboratory personnel would vary in number from eighty to more than five hundred and likely would work on fixed shifts, either day, evening, or night. (Most laboratories pay differentials—hourly increases in pay—for evening and night shifts.)

Independent Laboratories

If one chooses an independent (commercial) laboratory in which to work, one would expect a profit orientation, staff specialization, sophisticated instrumentation, and perhaps a production line approach to test performance. Patient contact would be limited, because specimens are obtained elsewhere and brought to the laboratory. Normally there would be little weekend or evening work, although more independent laboratories are operating twenty-four hours each day, seven days a week. In such cases, staffing needs would be met through rotating or fixed assignments.

Research

Research—both basic and applied—is an intriguing area of work and is chosen by a number of laboratorians. Basic research may involve, for example, the DNA sequencing of an epithelial cell membrane protein. Applied research may be concerned with evaluating the best chemotherapy regimen to use in treating leukemia or in understanding the immunologic changes that occur with aging. Research provides in-depth expertise in a small area of scientific inquiry; it also provides the opportunity to perform tests, analyze resultant data, and determine the significance of those data. Research may involve only a small amount of patient contact, and interaction with others is usually less frequent than in a health care setting.

Public Health

Another area in which laboratorians work is in public health. Here the identification of organisms causing outbreaks of infectious and communicable diseases is made. A variety of immunologic tests also are performed to determine one's prior exposure to mumps, measles, the HIV virus, or other microorganisms. Laboratory analyses for water purity, food safety, and environmental hazards are performed as well. Duties of personnel vary according to the needs of the public, and they are usually determined by a state department of health.

Blood Banks

In blood banks, such as those of the American Red Cross, blood is drawn, typed, and checked for any unexpected antibodies as well as for the absence of infectious agents such as the hepatitis or AIDS virus or syphilis spirochete. Usually there is a strong community spirit within blood banks, as physicians, nurses, and laboratorians work together to provide safe blood for citizens of the region.

Industry

Industry is attractive to laboratorians who have an entrepreneurial spirit. Here they can work in "research and development" (R & D) developing new tests or instrumentation, as a technical specialist assisting users who are having problems (e.g., troubleshooting instrumentation), or in sales.

Small Health Care Facilities

If one works in a clinic, health maintenance organization, or physician office laboratory, the kind and volume of testing depends on the size of the laboratory. The central laboratory of a large HMO, for example, might be very similar to that of a large hospital. However, the lab in a three-physician practice may offer only ten or twenty laboratory tests.

Organization of Laboratories

Laboratories are typically organized in a chain-of-command model. At the top are directors and administrators; in the middle are supervisory staff; and on the front line, performing the actual tests, are the staff technologists and technicians, together with others, including phlebotomists, obtaining blood. (See Figure 1 on the next page.)

Of course there are variations on this basic structure. In a hospital, for instance, the laboratory's organization depends on size,

Figure 1 An Organizational Structure Often Found in a Hospital Clinical Laboratory

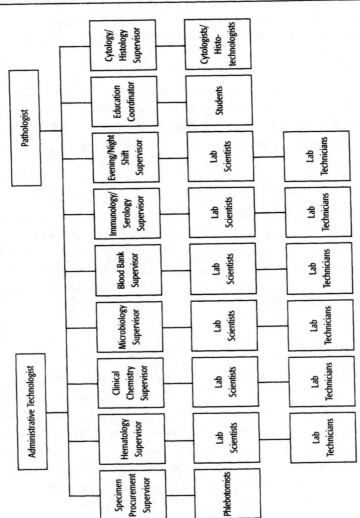

the types of patients it serves (pediatric, psychiatric, acute care), and its objectives. Most hospital laboratories are headed by a *medical director.* That individual usually is a physician specializing in pathology. In smaller hospitals, however, qualified nonphysicians, including clinical laboratory scientists and other personnel, assume administrative responsibility. They usually work with a consulting pathologist, who assumes medical responsibility.

In another model, usually larger, a physician (often a pathologist) holds the title *medical director,* and a clinical laboratory scientist holds the title *administrative director.* Under this arrangement, the physician is responsible for medical interpretive and consultative functions and for anatomical pathology tests, while the administrative director colleague actually manages the laboratory.

In the independent laboratory sector, it is quite common for nonphysician professionals to own, direct, and operate full-service laboratories.

According to standards affirmed by the American Society for Clinical Laboratory Science and under the shared medical and administrative director model, responsibilities are divided to draw most fully on each professional's expertise. In this model, the *physician director* is in charge of physician-patient services as well as a number of other important functions.

A physician director may also assist in establishing test protocols and policies. He or she will likely consult with medical personnel regarding tests and help interpret results and data. As team leader, the physician director will probably represent the clinical laboratory staff at conferences and may be expected to teach in primary and continuing education programs for medical and laboratory staff.

The *laboratory administrator* (often a clinical laboratory scientist) who, like the medical director, also reports to a senior member of the hospital administration, has responsibility for laboratory operations. He or she will prepare and maintain up-to-date laboratory procedures and quality control operations. Each category of service provided by the laboratory requires a procedural manual that the laboratory administrator prepares and keeps current. Supervision of other personnel, keeping work schedules in order, and ensuring proper performance of all procedures are also a part of the laboratory administrator's job duties. This requires proper orientation, training, and continuing education for all technical and supervisory staff. The administrator makes sure duties are assigned to capable personnel. Budgetary functions are usually part of the job, as are regular consultations with medical personnel.

The *technical supervisor* in each of the departments of the laboratory implements quality control practices to ensure accuracy and validity of test results and procedures. He or she prepares daily work schedules to provide adequate coverage and good use of available personnel. Supplies of reagents and other materials need to be commensurate with the workload, so the technical supervisor must be aware of each work area's needs. Employees must be trained and supervised to ensure that they follow laboratory policies, procedures, and safety practices.

Technical personnel include clinical laboratory scientists (medical technologists) and technicians. Duties performed by baccalaureate-level laboratory scientists (technologist) include those tests that require the exercise of independent judgment and responsibility with minimal supervision by the director or supervisor. Certain procedures like report results, equipment maintenance, record keeping, and other quality control requirements related to test performance would also fall to the trained laboratory scientist.

Another important duty is the direct personal supervision of trainees, technicians, and other supportive technical personnel employed by the laboratory.

Laboratory technicians, who normally possess a two-year technical degree, typically perform procedures that require limited exercise of independent judgment. They execute procedures under the supervision of a supervisor, or director, and they are expected to follow directions detailed in the procedural manual for each designated duty. Duties are assigned to technicians based on their qualifications and experience.

Advantages and Disadvantages of Working in Various Laboratory Settings

Today many options for the delivery of services exist. Some independent laboratories perform rare procedures on referral from physicians and hospital laboratories—procedures that hospitals and large group practices find too costly to offer. Examples include hair arsenic analysis, HLA-B27 typing to aid in the diagnosis of ankylosing spondylitis, or the identification of TA-4 marker for carcinoma. Other independent laboratories provide routine types of tests.

On the other hand, some hospitals refer many of their tests to commercial facilities and keep only an emergency laboratory operation, which is generally staffed round the clock and equipped to provide only a limited range of tests. Other hospital laboratories have entered the testing market quite aggressively. They not only do almost all their own tests; they also serve as referral laboratories for other health care institutions and act almost like independent laboratories. Test volume can vary from a few thousand tests a year (in a small physician office laboratory (POL) to millions of procedures (in large medical centers or independent facilities).

Although rapid specimen transit (by air or road courier) and computer technologies have made regional laboratories possible, not all testing can be done long-distance. The type of testing that a given facility offers depends significantly on the nature of the services provided and on the competition. Important factors for hospital laboratories are the patient caseload and whether or not the facility is a large, teaching hospital. A facility that serves predominantly cancer patients (an oncology hospital) or a psychiatric hospital would offer a menu of tests significantly different from each other, or from a multipurpose, acute care hospital. Similarly, a teaching hospital can be expected to offer a wider range of tests—including rare procedures—than a nonteaching hospital.

There is no laboratory that offers all employment advantages. As in every field, there are tradeoffs. Each type of facility has certain characteristics that may make it more or less attractive as a place to work.

Work Characteristics of Various Laboratory Settings

Small Hospital Laboratory attributes include: rotation among lab sections, making one a strong "generalist"; much patient contact; small test menu; small workforce; mandatory shift rotation and "taking call"; very strong patient care orientation; much interaction with other health care staff (optimizing a team spirit).

Teaching Hospital Laboratory attributes include: staff specialization; less patient contact; larger test menu; larger workforce; more new technology and instrumentation; usually fixed shift assignments; moderate patient care orientation; some interaction with other health care staff.

Independent (Commercial Laboratory) attributes include: staff specialization; no patient contact; profit-loss orientation (which may include bonuses); production line orientation; good advancement opportunities; limited contact with other health care professionals.

Research Laboratory attributes include: independent work; limited patient contact; opportunities to develop procedures and make decisions; flexible hours; development of in-depth knowledge of a specific area of inquiry; repetitive work; position may be dependent on grant money.

Public Health Laboratory attributes include: work heavily oriented to microbiology and immunology; very little patient contact; may involve routine testing; minimal weekend work; little interaction with other health professionals.

Blood Bank attributes include: strong commitment (organizational and individual) to providing safe blood and blood products for transfusion; specialized work; little direct patient contact; some donor contact; moderate interaction with other health care professionals, especially physicians and nurses.

Industry (example: development of or troubleshooting of new lab tests or instrumentation) attributes include: emphasis on scientific entrepreneurship and profit-making; may require knowledge of government regulations; work may be repetitive; no patient contact; limited interaction with other health care professionals; good opportunities for advancement.

Clinic or Physician Office Laboratory (having a limited practice) attributes include: limited test menu; may include other work, for example, X ray or record keeping; much patient contact; usually does not include shift or weekend work; strong interaction with clinic physicians or other staff.

Health Maintenance Organization (kinds and volume of testing related to size of HMO) attributes include: large HMO may have one central laboratory for complex tests and other satellite laboratories for routine tests; some patient contact; work may be streamlined. Small HMO has few tests; much like a small physician office laboratory.

Physician office laboratories and group practice laboratories span a wide range of characteristics. Some physician office laboratories offer only ten to twenty of the most common tests, are housed in a space the size of an apartment kitchen, and are staffed by one or two individuals—characteristically *not* laboratory professionals. At the other end of the continuum, large clinics (such as the Mayo Clinic) can surpass a medical school facility in test variety, the sophistication of the equipment, and the size and diversity of its staff.

Laboratory Safety

Clinical laboratory professionals are meticulously educated in the safe management and handling of toxic and infectious substances because this is an integral part of the work they do. Therefore, very reliable, safe procedures are in place and continually being improved upon. Precautions have intensified, and the universal precautions mandated by the Occupational Safety and Health Administration (OSHA) have drastically minimized any risk of accidental exposure to the laboratorian.

Over time, plastics and disposables have replaced much glassware. Chemical burns are extremely rare in health care laboratories because many reagents in use today are premixed and prepackaged.

Unpleasant odors, too, are rare. Thanks to changes in clinical laboratory practice itself, and to biosafety shields and ventilated hoods, today's clinical laboratory is likely to have a clean, astringent scent—if any at all.

Summary

Opportunities in clinical laboratory practice exist in a vast array of settings, both traditional and nontraditional. Depending upon one's interest and qualifications, there are opportunities for technical, supervisory, and management roles, as well as for a host of roles outside the laboratory itself. As today's health care industry continues to change in response to new economic pressures—including those pressures to control health care costs—and new discoveries in science, medicine, and clinical laboratory science itself are made, qualified clinical laboratory practitioners can look forward to an array of options within and outside of the conventional laboratory setting.

It is obvious that laboratory professionals can work in a variety of settings, although most work in hospitals. Other health-related sites include independent (commercial) laboratories, clinics, group practices, HMOs, blood banks, public health facilities, research laboratories, and industry.

In this chapter, duties and responsibilities of various laboratory personnel have been introduced. We can now move on to detailed descriptions of various laboratory personnel.

3

OVERVIEW OF LABORATORY
PERSONNEL

THE INDIVIDUALS WHO work in clinical laboratories are as varied as the laboratory settings themselves. The greatest numbers of laboratory personnel are those whom we called "clinical laboratory scientists," or "medical technologists."

The estimated number of laboratory personnel in the United States currently is at least 400,000 (see Table 6). Baccalaureate-level clinical laboratory scientists comprise a majority of the staffs of clinical laboratories in traditional health care settings.

In order to define the major players and their jobs in clinical laboratories, the following summary descriptions are provided. These summaries are taken in part from the 2001–2002 edition of the *Health Professions Career and Education Directory*, published by the American Medical Association, 515 North State Street, Chicago, IL 60610. Figure 2 also provides an overview of the routes to various laboratory careers.

Table 6 Estimated Numbers of Laboratory Practitioners by Year

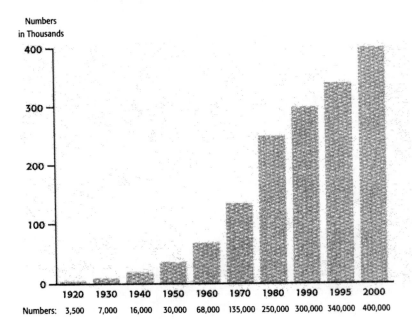

Numbers
in Thousands

	1920	1930	1940	1950	1960	1970	1980	1990	1995	2000
Numbers:	3,500	7,000	16,000	30,000	68,000	135,000	250,000	300,000	340,000	400,000

Kinds of Laboratory Personnel

Pathologist

Job Description

The majority of laboratory directors in the United States are pathologists, i.e., physicians with advanced training in the study of the nature, structure, and functional changes produced by diseases. There are two branches of pathology: anatomic pathology

Figure 2 The Usual Pathways to Laboratory Careers

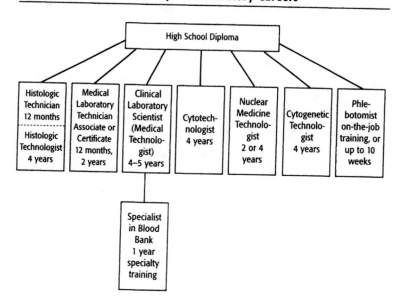

(AP) and clinical pathology (CP). Anatomic pathologists are those physician specialists who examine tissues from biopsies, surgeries, and autopsies both "macroscopically" (by eye) and microscopically. They determine whether the tissues are normal, infected, malignant, inflammatory, necrotic, or with other cellular changes. Pathologists may advise other physicians whether and how to treat those patients whose tissues they have examined.

The other branch of pathology is clinical pathology, sometimes called laboratory medicine. Clinical pathologists are responsible for directing the clinical laboratory or its sections and providing consultation to other physicians regarding test selection, interpretation of results, and diseases associated with various laboratory values. Clinical pathologists head research and development (R & D) efforts concerning new tests, methodologies, and instrumentation; they also teach residents, fellows, and other students. Salaries of pathologists vary. When in a residency program, their income is about $30,000 per year, and once in practice, salaries are usually in excess of $150,000 per year.

Employment Characteristics

Most pathologists are employed in hospital and medical center laboratories. Others are employed in private laboratories, large clinics or HMOs, forensic laboratories, and industry.

Educational Programs

To become a pathologist (anatomic or clinical) requires graduation from medical school plus a five-year residency program. Thus the usual number of years of schooling totals thirteen; four years in premedicine, four years of medical school, and five years in a residency program. Following this, most pathologists take a certification exam provided by the American Board of Pathology to certify them as "AP" or "CP" Some pathologists may choose to further their inquiry into a pathology subspecialty such as hematopathology or chemical pathology. In these cases, a one- or two-year fellowship is completed following the residency training, making the total educational experience fourteen or fifteen years.

Clinical Laboratory Scientist (Medical Technologist)

Clinical laboratory professionals (scientists educated at the baccalaureate level) perform analytic tests in clinical chemistry, microbiology, hematology, immunology, and other biological sciences. They provide data on blood, tissues, and fluids in the human body by using basic procedures as well as those requiring sophisticated instruments and complicated methodologies.

Job Description

Clinical laboratory scientists (technologists) perform many and varied analyses and use fine line discrimination in determining the correctness of results. They are able to recognize the interdependency of tests and have knowledge of physiologic and pathologic conditions affecting results in order to validate them. In most health care settings, they develop data that are used by physicians in determining the presence, extent, and, as far as possible, the causes of disease.

Clinical laboratory scientists assume responsibility for, and are held accountable for, accurate and timely results. They establish and monitor quality control programs and design or modify procedures as necessary.

Tests and procedures are performed or supervised by laboratory technologists in the clinical laboratory center in the major areas of hematology, coagulation, microbiology, immunohematology, immunology, clinical chemistry, and urinalysis. Subspecialty areas in which laboratorians work include such fields as molecular diagnostics, cytogenetics, fertility testing, flow cytometry, tissue typing, bone and skin banks, forensics, infection control, and others.

Employment Characteristics

The majority of clinical laboratory scientists are employed in hospital laboratories. Others are employed in commercial laboratories and clinics; HMOs; in the armed forces; in city, state, and federal health agencies; in industrial medical laboratories; in pharmaceutical houses; in public and private research programs; and as faculty of programs educating medical laboratory personnel. Salaries vary depending on the employer and geographic location. According to a 1999 survey published in *Laboratory Medicine*, the average entry-level salary for clinical laboratory scientists was $29,000, and the average manager's salary was $54,000.

The job market for baccalaureate-level laboratory technologists is more competitive, but it is projected to be good through the year 2006. More and more employers are realizing the importance of their backgrounds, scientific and technical skills, and sound judgment, together with their flexibility in being able to work in more than just one area.

Educational Programs

Clinical laboratory scientists (technologists) are graduates of baccalaureate programs that include a preprofessional component of two to four years and a professional component of one to two years. In colleges and universities that offer the preprofessional curriculum, but are not themselves accredited in laboratory science, students usually complete three years of school in a curriculum that is close to that of a premedical student or prepharmacy student. Prerequisite courses include general chemistry, general biology, organic and/or biochemistry, mathematics, microbiology, immunology, and perhaps computer science. Optional courses may include physics and statistics. Students then spend one year in an accredited "school" of medical technology, usually located in a hospital. This is often called a 3 + 1 program. In the final one-year portion, instruction and laboratory experiences are provided in the major laboratory areas.

In California the majority of medical technology programs are of the 4 + 1 model: 4 years in college and including a baccalaureate degree, followed by a 1-year clinical internship.

In colleges, universities, and medical centers that are themselves accredited in clinical laboratory science or medical technology, students usually spend two years in a preprofessional program and two years in a professional program. The first two years are spent in completing prerequisites in general chemistry, general biology, organic chemistry, mathematics, and microbiology. Again, the curriculum resembles that of a premedical or prepharmacy student. During the third year, students complete course work in immunology, anatomy, and physiology and may begin taking preclinical (introductory) laboratory courses in clinical chemistry, hematology, microbiology, and immunohematology. These introductory courses are usually conducted in student laboratories. Further courses in pathophysiology, management, and education may be provided, and in the final (fourth) year the actual hospital experience is shortened, for example, to fifteen to thirty weeks. In this 2 + 2 model, students start their laboratory work in year three, and the preprofessional and professional course work are integrated. This type of program is usually found in academic health science centers and medical schools.

Upon meeting specified qualifications and passing a national certification examination, these laboratory scientists (technologists) may be certified by one or more voluntary certifying agencies as "generalists," those who can perform in all of the major areas of clinical laboratories. Individuals are usually certified by the National Credentialing Agency for Laboratory Personnel (NCA) or the Board of Registry of the American Society of Clinical Pathologists (ASCP).

Cytotechnologist

Cytology is the study of the structure and the function of cells. Cytotechnologists are trained laboratory technologists who work with pathologists to detect changes in body cells that are important in the early diagnosis of cancer. Their work is done primarily with the microscope, and they screen slide preparations of body cells for abnormalities in structure, indicating either benign (noncancerous) or malignant (cancerous) conditions.

Job Description

Using special techniques, cytotechnologists prepare cellular samples for study under the microscope and assist in the diagnosis of disease by the examination of these samples. Cell specimens may be obtained from various body sites, such as the female reproductive tract (Pap smears), the oral cavity, the lung, or any body cavity shedding cells. Examination is made of abdominal fluids, thoracic fluids, central nervous system fluids, urine, sputum, and cells obtained by brushing the surfaces of various organs. Using the findings of cytotechnologists, the physician is able, in many instances, to diagnose cancer long before it can be detected by other methods. Cytologic techniques also are used to detect diseases involving hormonal abnormalities and other pathological disease processes. In recent years fine needle aspirations have been used to locate and identify tumors deeply seated in the body.

Employment Characteristics

Most cytotechnologists work in hospitals or in private laboratories, while others prefer to work on research projects or to teach. Employment opportunities are excellent, as the demand for trained cytotechnologists is high and is projected to remain high.

According to the "ASCP Salary Survey," published in the *ASCP Journal of Cytotechnology* (vol. 2, no. 3, 1997), the average hourly pay for cytotechnologists was $21.06 in 1997.

Educational Programs

The length of the cytotechnology program depends significantly on its organizational structure. In general, after completion of three years of prerequisite course work, at least one calendar year of structured professional instruction in cytotechnology is necessary to establish entry-level competencies.

Applicants should be well grounded in the biological sciences and in basic chemistry. This usually entails successful completion of at least twenty semester (thirty quarter) hours in the biological sciences, chemistry courses equaling or exceeding eight semester hours, and some mathematics.

The curriculum includes the historical background of cytology, cytology as applied in clinical medicine, cytology in the screening of exfoliate tumor cells, and areas of anatomy, histology, embryology, cytochemistry, cytophysiology, endocrinology, and inflammatory diseases.

Like in medical technology, some schools provide 2 + 2 curricula in cytotechnology, once again providing preclinical cytology courses in year three, and offering in-depth instruction in cell identification and fine needle biopsy examination.

Medical (Clinical) Laboratory Technician

Medical laboratory technicians (associate or certificate) perform many standardized procedures in the clinical laboratory under the direction of a qualified physician and/or clinical laboratory scientist.

Job Description

Medical laboratory technicians perform routine, uncomplicated procedures in the areas of hematology, serology, blood banking, urinalysis, microbiology, and clinical chemistry. These procedures involve the use of common laboratory instruments in processes where discrimination is clear, errors are few and easily corrected, and results of the procedures can be confirmed with a reference test or source within the working area. The technician has knowledge of specific techniques and instruments and is able to recognize factors that directly affect procedures and results. The technician also monitors quality control programs that have predetermined parameters.

Employment Characteristics

Some clinical laboratory technicians (CLTs) work in hospital laboratories, averaging a forty-hour week; many more technicians work in HMOs, clinics, and physician office laboratories.

Based on a 1999 survey published in *Laboratory Medicine*, the average entry-level salary was $22,000, and the average salary of technicians was $27,000 per year.

Educational Programs

Clinical laboratory technicians have two routes to choose in completing a CLT program. The first is the certificate program, which is usually twelve to fifteen months in length and often located at a vocational or technical institute or college. Here the curriculum includes areas of medical ethics and conduct, medical terminology, basic laboratory solutions and media, basic elements of quality control, blood collecting techniques, basic microbiology, hematology, serology, and immunohematology. A clinical practicum in a hospital or clinic laboratory concludes the certificate program.

The second route to becoming a clinical laboratory technician involves completion of an associate degree (CLT-AD) usually at a junior or community college. The period of education is usually two academic years. Courses are taught on campus and in affiliated hospital(s). The teaching laboratory on campus focuses on general knowledge and basic skills, understanding principles, and mastering procedures of laboratory testing. The clinical (hospital) courses include application of basic principles commonly used in the diagnostic laboratory. Technical instruction includes procedures in hematology, chemistry, microbiology, immunohematology, and immunology.

If one is planning to become a laboratory technician first and then take additional course work to become a medical technologist, it is recommended that the associate-level route be chosen. It may be difficult to transfer credits from a vocational or technical school to a college or university, whereas transfer of credits from a community or junior college can more easily be accomplished. In addition, due to regulations specified by the Clinical Laboratory Improvement Act of 1988, only associate-level CLTs may perform highly complex laboratory tasks. Thus, some certificate-level programs are converting to associate degree programs, or they are closing.

The "medical laboratory technician" title may also be designated for those who have graduated as Medical Laboratory Specialists in the armed forces (see Chapter 8).

Specialist in Blood Bank Technology

Job Description

Specialists in blood bank technology (SBB) demonstrate a superior level of technical proficiency and problem-solving ability in such areas as: (1) testing for blood group antigens, compatibility, and antibody identification; (2) investigating abnormalities such as hemolytic disease of the newborn, hemolytic anemias, and adverse responses to transfusion; (3) supporting physicians in transfusion therapy, including patients with coagulopathies or candidates for homologous organ transplant; (4) blood collection and processing, including selecting donors, drawing and typing blood, and performing pretransfusion tests to ensure the safety of the patient. Supervision, management, and/or teaching comprise a considerable part of the responsibilities of the specialist in blood bank technology.

Employment Characteristics

Specialists in blood banking work in many types of facilities, including community blood centers, hospital blood banks, university affiliated blood banks, transfusion services, and independent laboratories. They also may be a part of a university faculty. Qualified specialists may advance to supervisory or administrative positions, or move into teaching or research activities.

According to the American Medical Association's 2000–2001 edition of the *Health Professions Career and Education Directory*, entry-level salaries for blood banking specialists average between $32,000 and $42,000 per year.

Educational Programs

The minimum length of the SBB educational program is twelve consecutive months. Applicants must be certified in clinical laboratory science/medical technology and hold a baccalaureate degree from a regionally accredited college or university. If applicants are not certified in clinical laboratory science, they must possess a baccalaureate degree from a regionally accredited college or university with a major in one of the biological or physical sciences.

Each SBB educational program defines its own criteria for measurement of student achievement. The sequence of instruction meets the standards of the medical director and program director. The educational model and environment are designed to develop competence in all technical areas of the modern blood bank and transfusion services.

Nuclear Medicine Technologist

Nuclear medicine is the medical specialty that utilizes the nuclear properties of radioactive and stable nuclides to make diagnostic evaluations of the anatomic or physiologic conditions of the body and to provide therapy with unsealed radioactive sources.

Job Description

Nuclear medicine technologists (NMTs) perform in vivo and in vitro diagnostic procedures and utilize quality control techniques as part of a quality assurance program covering all procedures and products in the laboratory. They also apply their knowledge of radiation physics and safety regulations to limit radiation exposure, prepare and administer radiopharmaceuticals, and use radiation detection devices and other kinds of laboratory equipment that measure the quantity and distribution of radionuclides deposited in the patient or in a patient specimen.

Administrative functions may include supervising other nuclear medicine technologists, students, laboratory assistants, and various personnel; participating in ordering supplies and equipment; documenting laboratory operations; participating in departmental inspections conducted by various licensing, regulatory, and accrediting agencies; and scheduling patient examinations.

Employment Characteristics

The employment outlook in nuclear medicine technology is good. Opportunities may be found both in major medical centers and in smaller hospitals and independent imaging centers. Opportunities are also available for obtaining positions in clinical research, education, and administration.

According to a survey of the American Society of Radiologic Technologists, a staff nuclear medicine technologist averaged $45,000 each year and an administrator made $55,000 per year.

Educational Programs

The technical portion of a nuclear medicine program is one year in length. Institutions offering accredited programs may provide an integrated educational sequence leading to an associate or baccalaureate degree over a period of two or four years.

The curriculum includes patient care, nuclear physics, instrumentation and statistics, health physics, biochemistry, immunology, radiopharmacology, administration, radiation biology, clinical nuclear medicine, radionuclide therapy, and computer applications.

Histology Technician/Technologist

The responsibility of the histologic technician/technologist is to prepare sections of body tissue for examination by a pathologist.

This includes the preparation of tissue specimens of human and animal origin for diagnostic, research, or teaching purposes.

Job Description

Histotechnicians and histotechnologists process sections of body tissue by fixation, dehydration, embedding, sectioning, decalcification, microincineration, mounting, and routine and special staining. Histotechnologists are trained to perform all the functions of the histotechnician and in addition perform the more complex procedures for processing tissues. They identify tissue structures, cell components, and their staining characteristics and relate them to physiological functions; implement and test new techniques and procedures; make judgments concerning the results of quality control measures; and institute proper procedures to maintain accuracy and precision. Histotechnologists apply management and supervision principles when they function as supervisors and educational principles when they teach and supervise students.

Employment Characteristics

Most histologic technicians/technologists work in hospital and medical center laboratories, averaging a forty-hour week.

The median entry-level salary for histologic technologists is about $25,000 per year.

Educational Program

For histotechnicians, the program is twelve months. For the histotechnologist, a baccalaureate degree program of four years is required. This curriculum includes both instruction and practical experience in medical ethics, medical terminology, chemistry, anatomy, histology, histochemistry, quality control, instrumentation, microscopy, processing techniques, preparation of museum specimens, and record and administration procedures.

For the histologic technician level, the curriculum should be an integral part of a community college program culminating in an associate degree, and with courses including chemistry, biology, and mathematics. The baccalaureate-level program includes course work designed to prepare researchers, supervisors, and instructors with advanced capabilities.

Clinical Laboratory Specialist in Cytogenetics*

Cytogenetics is the study of heredity at the cellular level. Chromosomes, the condensed form of genetic material, are visible only during cell division. The standard representation of a single cell's chromosomes, paired and arranged in order and size, is called a "karyotype." By comparing the chromosomes from a sample of blood, fibroblasts, bone marrow, amniocytes, or other tissue to a standard pattern, the cytogenetic technologist establishes a karyotype and determines a cytogenetic diagnosis. This diagnosis is crucial for patient care and also may provide an indication that genetic counseling is required for family members.

Job Description

Clinical cytogenetics is the specialty devoted to the study of relationships among human diseases and chromosome alterations. At birth, chromosome changes can cause mental retardation and physical deformities. An example is Down's syndrome, in which an individ-

---

*Much of this material is taken from the Association of Genetic Technologists (AGT) description of the profession.

ual has an extra number 21 chromosome in each of his/her cells. Other chromosome changes, such as those found in the bone marrow cells of patients with leukemia, are acquired later in life and are found only in cells that are involved in the disease. An increasing number of diseases are being recognized as having a genetic component. Cytogenetic technologies therefore perform the tests that are essential for the diagnosis and treatment of chromosomal disorders.

Molecular biology uses a rapidly expanding group of technologies to explore the relationships among chromosomes, genes, and DNA. These areas include molecular biology, recombinant DNA and gene mapping techniques, gene product studies, and detection of gene rearrangements. Diseases diagnosed by molecular biology include cystic fibrosis, Duchene's muscular dystrophy, Huntington's disease, and myotonic dystrophy. Specific kinds of techniques include the polymerase chain reaction (PCR); Western, Northern, and Southern blots; heteroduplexing; and others. Technologists in this field use these tools to identify and localize the genes related to specific diseases in anticipation of possible treatments and even cures for some genetic disorders.

Employment Characteristics

Most cytogenetic technologists work in medical centers and academic health centers, averaging a forty-hour week. Entry-level salaries vary, but average $30,000 per year. A recent Web search showed some employers posting $1,000 signing bonuses. Competition for qualified personnel is very strong.

Educational Program

Entry into the field of cytogenetic technology requires a baccalaureate degree in clinical laboratory science/medical technology or in the biological sciences such as genetics, cytogenetic technology, or biology, as well as clinical experience, preferably with formal cytogenetic technology training.

Course work usually involves three to six months of formal course work including lecture and laboratory courses in medical cytogenetics, photography, and cytopreparatory techniques, followed by a six-month clinical internship.

Certification is accomplished by the National Credentialing Agency (NCA) as a Clinical Laboratory Specialist in Cytogenetics, or by the Canadian Society of Laboratory Technologists as a Registered Technologist in Cytogenetics. These credentials are internationally recognized standards of competence in the field.

Phlebotomist

Phlebotomists are those individuals who draw blood by venipuncture or micropuncture from patients for the purpose of chemical or cellular analysis. Most blood is obtained by venipuncture (blood withdrawn from a vein, usually in the arm), although tiny amounts of capillary blood from fingers or babies' heels can be used. In the past many phlebotomists were trained on the job (OJTs); now, short courses of four to ten weeks are provided in hospitals, community colleges, or technical and vocational schools.

Many phlebotomists work in hospitals, but others work in large clinics and HMOs. Often phlebotomists are the laboratory personnel who convey to patients the image of the laboratory; therefore it is important that they be highly professional in appearance and manner.

In 2000, entry-level phlebotomist salaries averaged $8.10 per hour ($16,000 annually), and the average salary for a phlebotomist was $11.80 per hour or $24,000 annually.

A high school diploma or equivalent is usually required to complete a phlebotomy program. Course work and/or training includes basic anatomy and physiology; medical terminology; specimen collection; anticoagulants; patient preparation; techniques; equipment; specimen processing and handling (specimen types, labeling, transport, and storage); safety; quality control; infection control; interpersonal relations; and professional ethics.

Generally a phlebotomy program includes at least 40 hours of didactic training followed by 120 clinical hours with a minimum performance of 100 successful venipunctures, 25 successful skin punctures, observation of 5 arterial punctures, and 8 hours of orientation in a full service laboratory.

Other Specialists

In addition to the previously mentioned laboratory personnel, there are other scientists and specialists who work in laboratories. These include clinical chemists, microbiologists, immunologists, and pathobiologists (Ph.D. level); master's-level personnel in these areas; and other specialists. These individuals are responsible for administering a laboratory section, performing research, and teaching. They may be clinical laboratory scientists with advanced degrees, or they may have biology, chemistry, or microbiology backgrounds with specialized training and education. They usually are employed in large hospitals, medical centers, and universities. Entry-level salaries vary by degree and experience, but may begin at $32,000 to $40,000 per year.

Others employed in laboratories include specialists who have advanced by way of holding a clinical laboratory science baccalaureate degree, with additional course work and experience. This group includes specialists in hematology, coagulation, chemistry, microbiology, immunohematology (blood banking), or immunology.

Other specialists are those who work in very defined areas such as molecular diagnostics, flow cytometry, cardiac catheterization, pulmonary function, and the like. They often receive their expertise by learning on the job following completion of a baccalaureate degree in clinical laboratory science. (See Chapter 4).

Yet another group, whose name is similar but whose educational preparation is different from cyto- or histotechnologists, is the histocompatibility technologist employed in organ donor and transplant centers. This individual determines maximum odds for transplanting donor tissues or organs successfully to recipients in need of skin, kidney, heart, lung, liver, pancreas, or other tissues and organs.

Practitioner Attributes

The following personal qualifications are similar for all practitioners in laboratory science. Additional aptitudes and abilities may be required for administrators, teachers, or researchers.

Intellectual Requirements

This science-based, investigative profession of laboratory science requires intelligence and sound problem-solving abilities. Interest and aptitude in science are essential, and competence in biology, mathematics, and basic chemistry are necessary. For the typical baccalaureate-level graduate, a clinical laboratory science major requires successful completion of courses in biology, anatomy, physiology, biochemistry, microbiology, and pathophysiology.

For supervisors, managers, and directors, requirements often include business and economics. Demands for cost containment and productivity and increased computerization have added human and fiscal management, computer science, and marketing to the knowledge base for laboratory administrators. And as health care competition and technology, together with new opportunities, extend the laboratory's reach beyond the hospital to very diverse care settings, good communications and interactive skills are essential.

Emotional Requirements

Clinical laboratory practitioners perform exacting laboratory procedures under considerable pressure; life-and-death situations join productivity demands to escalate the pressures under which they perform. Practitioners also must have an extremely high level of integrity and personal responsibility; patients' lives depend on their commitment to provide the highest quality of service.

Additional Requirements for Successful Practice

Recent accreditation standards by the National Accrediting Agency for Clinical Laboratory Sciences require that prospective students understand the "essential functions" required for a laboratory professional. Examples of some of these functions follow:

1. *Communication Skills.* Must be able to communicate effectively in written and spoken English; comprehend and respond to both formal and colloquial English—person-to-person, by telephone, and in writing; and assess nonverbal as well as verbal communication.

2. *Locomotion.* Must be able to move freely from one location to another in physical settings such as the clinical laboratory, patient areas, corridors, and elevators.

3. *Small Motor Skills.* Must have sufficient eye-motor coordination to allow delicate manipulations of specimens, instruments, and tools; must be able to grasp and release small objects (test tubes, microscope slides); twist and turn dials/knobs (for a microscope, balance, spectrophotometer); and manipulate other laboratory materials (reagents and pipettes) in order to complete tasks.

4. *Other Physical Requirements.* Must have the ability to lift and move objects of at least twenty pounds and have a sense of touch and temperature discrimination.

5. *Visual Acuity.* Must be able to identify and distinguish objects macroscopically and microscopically and read charts, graphs, and instrument scales.

6. *Safety.* Must be able to work safely with potential chemical, radiologic, and biologic hazards (to include the use of universal precautions) and to follow prescribed guidelines for working with potential mechanical or electrical hazards.

7. *Professional Skills.* Must be able to follow directions and work independently and with others and under time constraints; prioritize requests and work concurrently on at least two different tasks; and maintain alertness and concentration during a normal work period.

8. *Stability.* Must possess the psychological health required for full utilization of abilities and be able to recognize emergency situations and take appropriate actions.

9. *Affective (Valuing) Skills.* Must show respect for self and others and project an image of professionalism, including appearance, dress, and confidence.
10. *Application Skills.* Must be able to apply knowledge, skills, and values learned from previous course work and life experiences to new situations.

Clinical laboratories employ a wide variety of personnel, ranging in background from doctorally prepared scientists to on-the-job trained phlebotomists or aides. The largest group employed are clinical laboratory scientists (medical technologists) who comprise about one-half of all persons found in traditional health care settings. These individuals continue to lead the practice of laboratory science and to provide accurate and timely laboratory information to aid in disease prevention, diagnosis, and treatment, together with the monitoring of patient care.

4

OPPORTUNITIES WITHIN
LABORATORY SCIENCE

CHAPTERS 2 AND 3 have described the work sites and job responsibilities of various laboratory personnel working for the most part
in health care organizations such as hospitals and medical centers.
However, once a person has acquired a baccalaureate degree based
on a solid grounding in laboratory science, he/she will have many
job opportunities, not only in traditional care settings, but elsewhere as well.

Where the Jobs Are

Figure 3 that follows shows actual positions taken by graduates of
the University of Minnesota Bachelor of Science program. This
figure depicts jobs inside and outside of health. It is arranged by
the following groupings:

- hospitals and medical centers
- health care or government agencies
- health care administration
- management information systems
- health maintenance organizations
- consultantships
- reference/commercial laboratories
- veterinary medicine
- working abroad
- humanitarian work
- education
- other professional routes
- industry
- research

Altogether, Figure 3 includes more than 130 career opportunities for individuals holding a bachelor's degree in laboratory science/medical technology. Some of these positions can be acquired through additional experience, for example, after five years one can become a section supervisor. Others require additional formal education, such as that for becoming a physician or academician (a faculty member in a college or university).

Figure 3 includes examples of what many laboratorians have achieved, using their education in laboratory science as a "springboard" for careers within the field itself, together with other careers in basic and applied science, research, administration, industry, and other areas.

Hospital/Medical Center

Explanations for some of the positions listed in Figure 3 should be made. Starting from the upper left column and considering work

Figure 3 Career Opportunities in Clinical Laboratory Science

Hospital/Medical Center:
Laboratory Areas
Andrology/Fertility Testing
Blood Bank
Bone Marrow
Cell Markers
Chemistry
Coagulation
Components—Transfusion Service
Computer Science
Cytogenetics
Cytology/Histology
Drug Analysis (Toxicology)
Endocrinology
Flow Cytometry
Forensic Science
Genetics
Hematology
Immunology
Immunopathology
Infection Control
Microbiology
Molecular Diagnostics
Mycology
Nuclear Medicine
Outpatient and/or Clinic Lab
Parasitology
Pathology—Anatomical (Surgical, Autopsy)
Phlebotomy/Specimen Processing
Photography/Illustration
Platelet Studies
Quality Assurance
Serology
Skin or Bone Bank
STAT Laboratory
Tissue Typing
Transplant Services
Transfusion Technical Speciality
Urinalysis
Virology

Health Care Agency/Government
Administrator for Veteran's Administration Center
Biometrist
Crime Laboratory Scientist
Department of Health—Educator
Department of Health—Proficiency Test Consultant
Employee Recruiter/Placement Officer
Environmental Health Inspector
Environmental Pathology Technologist
Fraud Investigator
Health Management Organization—Health Educator
JCAHO Survey Team Member/CAP Inspector
Military Service—Armed Forces, ROTC, National Guard
NASA Mission Specialist
Patient Educator
Private Investigator FBI/Special Agent (Forensic Lab)

Health Care Administration
Clinic Manager/Administrator
Coder-Abstractor (Business or Medical Records Office)
Emergency Medical Services Coordinator
Financial Manager/Planner
Group Practice Administrator
Hazardous Waste Coordinator
Health Care Administrator
Health Insurance Administrator
Health Policy Analyst
Health Promotion Coordinator
Hospital Personnel Director
Hospital Quality Assurance Coordinator
Infection Control Officer→ Epidemiologist
Laboratory Supervisor→ Laboratory Administrator
Laboratory Utilization Review Coordinator
Long-Term Care Administrator
Mental Health Administrator
Purchaser (Laboratory/Hospital/Medical Center)
Staffing Coordinator (Laboratory, Health or Home Care)

Clinical Laboratory Scientist (Staff Medical Technologist)

Management Information Systems
Biometrician
Director-Division of Biometry
Installer/Educator
Programmer
Systems Analyst

Health Maintenance Organization
Laboratory Supervisor→ Administrator

Consultant to Physician Office Laboratories
Reference/Commercial Laboratory Scientist
Veterinary Medicine Laboratory Technologist
Working Abroad

Humanitarian Work
Medical Missionary Work
Peace Corps
Project HOPE, others

Education
Allied Health Dean/Health Sciences Administrator
Education Coordinator→Program Director
Educator of Students in Clinical Settings
Faculty Member in CLS/CLT/Cyto/SBB, Other Programs
Higher Education Administrator
Instructor in Vet. Med., Allied Health, or Other Programs
Medical Community Services Program Coordinator

Other Professional Routes
Accounting
Counseling Psychology
Dentistry
Health Radiation Science
Law (e.g. Patent Attorney)
Legislative Arena-Politician, Lobbyist, Regulations Writer
Medical Physics/Engineering
Medicine
Optometry
Pharmacy
Public Health
Veterinary Medicine

Industry (U.S. or International)
Advisor in Development of, or Inventor of Lab Tests
Biomedical Specialist in Occupational Health
Cell Culture Consultant
Computer Consultant
Director of Marketing
Editor/Writer-Medical Publications
Food Technologist→Quality Assurance Manager
Health Care Reimbursement Coordinator
Health Promotion and Education Specialist
Industrial Hygiene Specialist
Installation Specialist
Insurance Underwriter
Manager-Health Claims Administration
Medical Claims Reviewer/Auditor/ Insurance Processor
Medical Consultant (TV/Movie Industry)
Medical Fee Analyst-Insurance
Owner/Director of Employee Placement Service
Product Specialist
Quality Control/Quality Assurance Monitor/Director
Research and Development Technologist/Director
Research Scientist
Risk Management Representative-Insurance
Salesperson
Technical Representative

Research: Basic and Applied
Research Assistant
Associate Scientist/Scientist
Director of Research
Clinical Trial Coordinator

in a large hospital or medical center, the opportunities for specialization are great, as demonstrated by thirty-eight entries within this category.

The first category, "andrology" or fertility testing, is the study of reproduction, specifically, in bringing about the fertilization of an ovum and sperm to produce an embryo, then a fetus, and ultimately a newborn. Fertility testing and andrology laboratories often are seen in the reproductive units of large medical centers. Here laboratorians and scientists attempt to help infertile couples bear children, and their success increases yearly.

The usual laboratory areas of a hospital include the blood bank, chemistry, coagulation, hematology, immunology, microbiology, and serology. In addition, other hospital or medical center laboratory specialty areas may include the following:

Bone Marrow Laboratory. Personnel in this area differentiate blood cells formed in the bone marrow, which can be removed by bone marrow biopsy and then stained and examined for cellular normality or malignancy. Other bone marrow specialty laboratories harvest, process, and store bone marrow tissue from donors to be used for bone marrow transplants.

Cell Markers. Cell markers are used for the identification and quantification of malignant, neoplastic, and normal cells within the bone marrow. Using cell size, granularity, and fluorescent intensity of monoclonal antibodies, cell lineage can be determined. Such precise information is valuable in evaluating lymphoid or myeloid malignancies. In addition, because specific cell proteins on white cells (leukocytes) act as antigenic determinants, identification of specific cell types—such as leukemic and lymphoma cells—can be made using monoclonal antibodies, specific markers of heavy and light chains of immunoglobulins, as well as the use of flow cytometry.

Components-Transfusion Service. Blood can be separated into its components—plasma, red cells, white cells, and platelets—and further fractionated into plasma subcomponents such as factor VIII. Other blood components are also available for transfusion. Experts in component therapy obtain, test, transport, store, and provide blood and its products as needed for surgery, therapy, or prophylactic purposes. Many of these personnel work not only in hospital laboratories, but also for agencies such as the American Red Cross, whose goals include the distribution of safe blood and blood products for the nation.

Computer Science. Many laboratories are computerized and may employ laboratory specialists who write programs, "debug" packaged programs, and provide the necessary computer interfaces among the laboratory, patient units, patient records, and the like.

Cytogenetics. (Also described in Chapter 3.) This is the science of the number, structure, and abnormalities of chromosomes. Laboratory professionals who specialize in cytogenetics usually hold a baccalaureate degree and spend at least six months to one year learning how to grow cells containing chromosomes, separating and grouping chromosomes by position, and locating and identifying abnormalities. The result is a karyotype, a picture of the paired chromosomes, with specific abnormalities delineated. The field of cytogenetics is becoming increasingly important in identifying prenatal (fetal) abnormalities such as Down's syndrome, together with other disease states such as various leukemias. For example, the "Philadelphia chromosome" is associated with 85 percent of patients with chronic myelogenous leukemia and represents the translocation of genetic material from the long arm of chromosome 22 on to chromosome 9.

Cytology and Histology. These are areas of anatomic pathology in which body cells and tissues are prepared, stained, and examined for abnormalities. Tissue sections used usually include materials from biopsies, surgeries, and autopsies.

Drug Analysis. Sometimes called "toxicology" or "drug monitoring," this is the science involved in identifying and quantifying drugs in a person's blood, urine, or gastric contents. In crime-related cases, drug analysis also may be performed on hair, skin, or fingernail scrapings. Drugs analyzed may be substances of abuse such as barbiturates, opiates, or amphetamines. Examples of therapeutic drugs include lithium (to treat manic depressive disorders) or digoxin (to treat cardiac arrhythmias). The latter two drugs are measured to obtain a level of therapeutic effectiveness, but non-toxicity to the body.

Endocrinology. This chemistry subsection quantitates various hormones, such as insulin, thyroid hormones T_3, T_4, TSH), cortisol, growth hormone, 17-hydroxyprogesterone, and others associated with maintaining homeostasis (equilibrium) within the body.

Flow Cytometry. This is the area concerned with determining subsets of white cells. A flow cytometer operates by causing cells in a fluid stream to pass single file (hydrodynamic focusing) through a beam of light, usually a laser. Fluorochromes present on or in the cell absorb the laser light and re-emit the light at a lower energy and longer wavelength, giving fluorescence. The photons of light that are scattered and emitted by the cells following their interaction with the laser beam, are separated into constituent wavelengths by a series of filters and mirrors. Collection of light scattering events along the axis of laser beam (at 360 degrees) is known as forward angle light scatter and is roughly proportional to the size of the cells. Electronic gating can then be used to analyze selected subpopulations, such as T and B cells.

Forensic Science. Here personnel in county, state, and national crime laboratories attempt to determine the cause of death in any case that is not "natural." This includes the performance of an autopsy and also may involve blood typing, histocompatibility testing, DNA testing, drug analysis, and other laboratory procedures to help determine not only cause of death, but perhaps who might be responsible for that which is criminal in nature.

Genetics (Biochemical or Molecular). Specialized genetics or biochemical laboratories (also called molecular diagnostics laboratories) analyze for "errors of biochemical metabolism." Specific diseases such as phenylketonuria, tyrosinemia, infant galactosemia, glycogen storage disease, or Tay-Sachs disease may be diagnosed by abnormal levels of various amino acids, organic acids, mono and disaccharides, mucopolysaccharides, and abnormal oligosaccharides. Other diseases such as cystic fibrosis, Huntington's disease, or Fragile-X syndrome can be diagnosed using molecular techniques such as PCR, or Southern, Northern, and Western blot analyses.

Immunopathology. This involves testing tissue biopsies and blood for pathologic components. Tests include those for antinuclear antibodies, immune complexes, complement, and components of complement.

Infection Control. This is concerned with maintaining a health care institution that is as free of infectious agents as possible. Investigation is made of nosocomial (hospital-acquired) infections, loss of sterility of usually sterile items (such as surgical forceps), and outbreaks of infections in units such as the nursery. Infection control practitioners usually include laboratorians, nurses, and physicians.

Mycology. This is a subspecialty of microbiology and involves the identification of fungi that cause cutaneous (skin), subcutaneous (tissue), and systemic or organ diseases. Pathogenic fungi include examples such as *Trichophyton*, which causes athlete's foot; *Candida*, which is a yeast involved in oral infections; and *Histoplasma*, which causes a lung disease similar to tuberculosis.

Nuclear Medicine. (Also described in Chapter 3.) Here, and as an example, a patient may be given a radioactive substance, such as iodine, and after a short interval, be checked for the localization of that radionuclide by way of a scintillation image. The scintillation image can be interpreted as representing a malignant or benign tumor. (This is an "in vivo" test.)

Outpatient and/or Clinic Laboratories. These may be found within a hospital or medical center to provide basic and timely laboratory tests for outpatient or clinic patients.

Parasitology. This is a subsection of microbiology concerned with the identification of parasites. Examples of parasites include *Plasmodia*, which causes malaria; *Giardia*, which causes diarrhea; or *Taenia*, a tapeworm of infected pork.

Pathology. This area usually includes anatomic and clinical pathology, histology, and cytology, positions that have been described in Chapter 3.

Phlebotomy/Specimen Processing. In many health care centers, phlebotomists obtain blood samples by venipuncture or skin puncture.

These specimens are then processed in a central area. Processing involves separation of plasma or serum (the fluid portion) from red cells. This is usually followed by separating (aliquoting) plasma or serum into smaller samples to be distributed to a number of laboratories. Some samples may be stored (by refrigeration or freezing) for "batching" and tested at specified times.

Photography/Illustration. Some institutions have their own photographers and illustrators to assist in preparing pictures and illustrations for articles for publication as well as for education or patient visualization. They usually photograph entire specimens and microscopic stained sections of specimens to assist in diagnosis, as well as for the documentation of tissue and cellular abnormalities.

A Platelet Studies Laboratory. This is a subspecialty of both blood banking and coagulation and involves testing platelets from patients with drug-induced immune thrombocytopenia (low platelets), posttransfusion purpura (bruising), or autoimmune thrombocytopenia purpura (low platelets from self-made antibodies) to determine the reasons for these bleeding or "oozing" conditions.

Quality Assurance (QA). Certain laboratory personnel may be designated to plan, implement, and oversee quality assurance programs for the laboratory and the institution. To do so, they set standards for the organization and establish corrective actions when these standards have not been met. Within a laboratory, quality assurance involves the selection and use of laboratory methods; the performance of tests and reporting of test results;

the collection and handling of specimens; the selection, calibration, and maintenance of equipment; the selection and use of reagents, controls, standards, and supplies; personnel decisions; and the development, documentation, use, and review of all testing processes.

Skin or Bone Bank. Most hospitals have blood banks. A few specialized health care institutions also may have skin banks and bone banks whose products are used in skin grafts (such as for those severely burned) or bone grafts (for those with serious fractures or bone degeneration). The usual sources of skin and bone graft materials are cadavers.

STAT Laboratory. The word *STAT* means "immediately." It is used to identify an emergency situation. Thus, STAT laboratories may be established within or near areas where emergency situations are frequently encountered: the emergency room, operating room, or neonatal (newborn) nursery.

Tissue Typing. When an organ such as kidney, heart, liver, or pancreas is transplanted, specialized testing (sometimes called "histocompatibility testing") must always be performed to determine compatibility between the recipient and the organ. Most tissue typing involves three kinds of testing: serologic, mixed lymphocyte reactions, and cytotoxic T-cell typing. The intent is the same as for blood transfusions: to minimize rejection of the transplanted organ by matching organ tissue and recipient tissue.

Tissue typing also may involve HLA—human leukocyte antigen testing—to determine the association between a certain white cell antigen and particular disease, such as the HLA-B27 type and ankylosing spondylitis (rheumatic arthritis of the spine).

Transplant Services. In association with the blood bank and tissue typing laboratory, an institution may have designated personnel who assist in transplantation procedures. "Perfusionists" (sometimes called "extracorporeal technologists") are persons skilled in maintaining a patient's circulatory and/or respiratory function, usually during extensive surgery. Often they also maintain the viability of an organ between the time of removal from the donor to transplantation within the recipient.

Virology. Virology laboratories are found in about 20 percent of all hospitals. Personnel in these laboratories are responsible for identifying viruses causing acute viral infections such as influenza, as well as determining a patient's immune status to a particular virus (such as polio, measles, or mumps). Since viruses will not grow on ordinary laboratory media, they must be grown in tissue culture. Other techniques used in the virology laboratory include tissue culture neutralization, counterimmunoelectrophoresis, hemagglutination inhibition, immunofluorescence, and others.

Health Care Agency/Government

Under the title "Health Care Agency/Government," fifteen different positions are listed, ranging from an administrator for the Veteran's Affairs Medical Center to a private investigator for the FBI. The government employs laboratory personnel in the clinical laboratories of VA hospitals and as administrators and educators within its many agencies.

"Biometrists" are those scientists who analyze mathematical and statistical data from biology, medicine, and public health and forecast the implications of these data in laboratory testing or health care usage. Their emphases include biostatistics, experimental design and analysis, health statistics, clinical trials, and computerized data management. Often biometrists are laboratory scientists with additional course work and experience in statistics, computer science, logic, informatics, and public health.

Crime laboratories—federal, state, and county—employ laboratorians to analyze body fluids, including blood, urine, gastric contents, and semen, as well as other substances such as skin, nails, or hair from crime-related deaths or injuries. Some laboratorians work directly as FBI investigators, special agents, or scientists.

State departments of health also employ laboratory scientists to investigate water and air purity, outbreaks of food poisonings, or communicable diseases. A title such as "environment health inspector" may be used for this laboratory professional.

JCAHO and CAP are acronyms for the Joint Commission on the Accreditation of Healthcare Organizations and the College of American Pathologists. Both groups inspect laboratories for purposes of accreditation. Each employs laboratorians as laboratory inspectors. With the implementation of the Clinical Laboratory Improvement Amendments of 1988, other laboratory evaluations are occurring as well. Again, laboratory personnel at the baccalaureate level are often employed as inspectors.

Also of interest are opportunities in the U.S. space program. To become a NASA Mission Specialist Astronaut Candidate requires a master's degree and two years experience in one's field of interest, such as hematology or immunology, plus other qualifications specified by NASA.

One also can become a patient educator at the local, state, or national level. This experience may require some public health courses and fieldwork experience.

Administrative Positions

Health care administration includes nineteen titles for which laboratory personnel are qualified. To become a laboratory section supervisor usually requires experience; to become a laboratory director often requires an advanced degree, such as the M.A., M.B.A., or Ph.D degree.

Other positions seen on the career opportunities diagram include manager of a clinic, or a coder in the business office. For the latter, one "codes" tests for billing, knowing the nature of the tests and the patient's condition. One also may serve as a service specialist, personnel director, coordinator of emergency services (such as a triage coordinator in the emergency room), or financial manager. When physicians work together in a group practice (usually including five or more physicians), a coordinator may serve as the overall administrator of that practice.

Since health care institutions and related industries are under increasing surveillance for the ways they dispose of waste, laboratory professionals are increasingly taking positions as coordinators of waste removal, especially in handling hazardous wastes such as needles, syringes, microbiologic media, specimens, plasticware, and reagents. These hazardous substances may be first autoclaved (heated to high temperatures with steam under pressure) within their institutions, and then disposed of in appropriate areas. Because laboratory personnel are familiar with potential hazards, they are excellent choices as managers of waste removal units.

With additional training, for example an M.B.A. or Ph.D. degree, a laboratorian may become an administrator of a hospital, clinic, HMO, as well as an officer in an organization dealing with health insurance or health policy decisions.

In the past, coordinators of health promotion programs have come from the professions of nursing or public health. Nevertheless, opportunities are available for laboratorians in health promotion. Laboratory personnel understand what cholesterol is, its derivations, and the effects it has on hardening of the arteries; what carbon monoxide (from smoking) does to hemoglobin; as well as the effects of exercise on muscle and its enzymes. Therefore, clinical laboratory professionals are excellent resource persons for health promotion programs.

Laboratory quality assurance managers can go on to become hospital quality assurance coordinators or officers. Likewise, many laboratorians who specialize in microbiology can become infection control officers, and with additional course work, epidemiologists (those trained to determine the specific cause[s] of outbreaks of infection, of toxic poisoning, or of diseases of recognized origin). An epidemiologist also may be involved in studying the factors determining the frequency and distribution of disease in a population, such as the association of cancer with environmental or industrial "carcinogens" (agents that cause cancer, such as asbestos or DDT).

Utilization review (UR) is a form of health care review carried under the Social Security Act of 1965. The intent of utilization review is to ensure the medical necessity and appropriateness of care, and it involves the establishment of review committees to examine inappropriate care. Laboratorians are especially effective in utilization review when they observe misuse of testing (such as ordering too many tests), or inappropriate patterns of testing (such as certain physicians wanting twenty-test profiles or "batteries" of tests that are unnecessary).

Within the category of health care administration, a laboratory professional may assume the position of staffing coordinator, that is, in determining appropriate numbers and levels of practitioners. Laboratory professionals are well known for their organizational abilities. Therefore determining staffing patterns for a medical unit (including scheduling and establishing a proper mix of employees), can be a positive outgrowth of one who is first a laboratory staffing coordinator.

Other Opportunities

Management information systems (the management of data and information through the use of computers) encompasses positions ranging from computer programmer to director of a biometry section.

Health maintenance organizations (HMOs) employ laboratory personnel not only as staff members, supervisors, and directors, but also as administrators. This area (the HMO) is one of the most rapidly growing in health care and is intended to promote good health as well as care for those with diseases.

Laboratorians may choose to work as consultants, for example, in physician office laboratories in establishing and monitoring quality control, in instrument maintenance, in implementing procedures for safety, in billing, and in other matters important to these practices. Other consultantships include those in public health laboratories, clinics, and HMOs.

Reference (commercial or independent) laboratories hire significant numbers of laboratory personnel. In these independent laboratories, samples are brought in for analysis. Such laboratories may specialize in areas like drug analysis, virology, or cytology. Or they may provide a full range of laboratory services. Their representatives serve as consultants to assist small laboratories in establishing and verifying new procedures, quality assurance, and the like.

Veterinary medicine clinics and zoos employ laboratory technologists to perform hematologic, chemical, microbiologic, and immunologic analyses very similar to those that are available to humans. Sometimes additional training is needed (for example, in hematology—birds have red cells that have nuclei; mature human red cells do not have nuclei). Most often the equipment, supplies, and reagents seen in veterinary medicine clinics are similar to those seen in human clinic laboratories. Zoos also employ laboratory personnel, whose work is very diverse and challenging, such as in obtaining and analyzing blood from a lion or a whale.

Some laboratorians choose to work abroad, especially in research laboratories and pharmaceutical and product development companies. The International Red Cross employs personnel for its blood banks, and other laboratorians serve as educators. If involved in humanitarian endeavors (as a missionary, or working with the Peace Corps) they may set up laboratories and teach, as well as perform analyses. Project HOPE is devoted to international educational endeavors and uses laboratory professionals as both short-term and long-term consultants in various parts of the world.

Education is a popular route for laboratorians to take. All NAACLS accredited laboratory science programs have a program director or education coordinator in charge. Many universities and health science centers have faculty members who teach professional courses. Most within this group have advanced degrees, and they are responsible not only for teaching, but also research and service within their academic units. Other programs, including CLT, cytotechnology, nuclear medicine, cytogenetics, or the specialist in blood bank curricula, also require program coordinators and faculty who are laboratory professionals devoted to teaching.

Laboratory science faculty members may go on to become administrators, for example, as deans of schools of allied health or as provosts and presidents of colleges and universities. Finally, under education, laboratorians may serve in community service programs as coordinators or staff members.

Other professional routes are attractive as well. Since the laboratory science curriculum is quite similar to that required by other pre–health care professional students, laboratory science graduates can go on to complete programs in medicine, dentistry, pharmacy, and veterinary medicine. While in these schools, students with a laboratory background often work part-time in various laboratories, ensuring a good income while enrolled in these other professional curricula.

Baccalaureate-level laboratorians may choose accounting, law, engineering, medical physics or radiation science, optometry (concerning eye examinations and prescriptions), public health, or other health-related professions.

In industry, energetic and entrepreneurial laboratorians assist in developing new tests and equipment, in marketing and selling products, in serving as technical resource persons (troubleshooting test procedures or instruments), and in researching new methodologies. They also have been employed by insurance companies, worked as editors or managers of medical publications, in food technology, and in installing equipment. Others are employed as consultants for the movies or television. Many work in insurance in various roles, and others own their own companies such as in temporary placement services (providing short-term personnel to those needing them).

Finally, research—both basic and applied—attracts at least one of every ten laboratorians. Researchers may work as staff research technologists, scientists, or as directors of programs.

It can be seen that many and varied job opportunities exist for laboratory professionals. They can choose to work within health care or engage in other endeavors. Their laboratory background suits them well for new opportunities. Clinical laboratory professionals possess the concrete scientific and technical skills, organizational abilities, and the follow-through necessary to be successful in any new venture.

5

BECOMING A LABORATORY PROFESSIONAL

To BECOME A laboratory professional requires intelligence, a commitment to working hard in school, a desire to help humankind, and a love of science. Use the following checklist to help you determine whether you may be suited to a career as a laboratory professional.

Personal Checklist

Yes No

☐ ☐ 1. It is important to me to have a career that involves helping others.

☐ ☐ 2. To my friends, family, and teachers, I am known to be a person of honesty and integrity.

☐ ☐ 3. I have good manual dexterity and can translate thinking skills into doing skills.

Yes No

☐ ☐ 4. I like a certain amount of order or structure in the work that I do.

☐ ☐ 5. I am able to plan and carry out activities with little supervision.

☐ ☐ 6. It is important to me to have a sense of accomplishment (achievement) for the work I do.

☐ ☐ 7. In a work situation, I prefer to be busy and use my time well.

☐ ☐ 8. I enjoy solving problems.

☐ ☐ 9. I am capable of working effectively in stressful situations.

☐ ☐ 10. I am able to prioritize and carry out tasks when given several of them to do at the same time.

☐ ☐ 11. I have good communication skills.

☐ ☐ 12. I enjoy using various instruments (such as microscopes), as well as computers.

☐ ☐ 13. I like to know why things happen and what causes certain biologic conditions to occur.

☐ ☐ 14. I enjoy learning new ways of doing things.

☐ ☐ 15. I wish to play a significant role in finding the causes of disease and in helping people to improve their lives.

☐ ☐ 16. I like and do well in science courses, especially biology.

☐ ☐ 17. I know that work in clinical laboratory science involves testing blood and other biological substances for their cellular, chemical, or biological components.

☐ ☐ 18. I understand that with a degree in laboratory science, I can work in laboratories in hospitals, clinics, research, veterinary medicine, industry, and a number of other areas.

Yes No

□ □ 19. I know that in laboratory science I will use the latest scientific discoveries in my work.

□ □ 20. Following high school, I am willing to spend two to five years (depending on the program chosen) to prepare for a profession in laboratory science.

□ □ 21. Following high school, I would enjoy studying science and other courses needed to prepare for a profession in laboratory science.

□ □ 22. In college, I understand that to enter a professional program in clinical laboratory science (medical technology), I will need to demonstrate my academic abilities by earning good grades.

□ □ 23. I understand that a degree in laboratory science/medical technology can be the basis for graduate work in laboratory science as well as in the biological and physical sciences, medicine, dentistry, law, education, and administration.

□ □ 24. I know that in some settings, laboratory personnel interact with patients with infectious diseases, together with biologic fluids from these patients, but that precautions for safety are well established.

□ □ 25. I like medically related activities, but not one hundred percent direct patient contact.

□ □ 26. I understand that laboratory science is a profession based on the team concept in which health care providers work together to achieve positive outcomes.

□ □ 27. I understand that the starting salaries for clinical laboratory personnel are usually comparable to those of other allied health professionals.

Yes No

☐ ☐ 28. I recognize that in this profession, I may have to work evening, night, or weekend shifts, depending on the work setting I choose.

☐ ☐ 29. I am willing to treat all patients and their families equally and humanely—with respect and care.

☐ ☐ 30. As a health care professional, I will be able to keep all patient or client information in the strictest confidence.

___ ___ Total

To score this assessment instrument, give two points for a yes response to items 2, 3, 5, 8, 9, 10, 12, 16, 17, and 22. These items have been chosen by forty laboratory educators as the ten key statements for a potential student to become a successful laboratory scientist. Give one point to a yes response for each of the other twenty items. If your total score is 30 or more, you are an excellent candidate for becoming a successful clinical laboratory professional. If you score from 20–29, you are a good candidate. If you score 19 or less, you should probably investigate other career options.

The checklist also can be grouped in two ways: knowledge of self (items 1–16), and knowledge of the field (items 17–30). Both are important in choosing a career, especially one in laboratory science.

High School Highlights

The usual high school education consists of four years of secondary school studies beginning with the ninth grade and concluding with completion of the twelfth grade of study. Courses of instruction in a secondary (high school) school curriculum are usually measured in terms of *units*. A unit is defined as one year's work on a single subject. Most high school students will study the course of English during each of the four years in attendance, thereby accumulating four units in that subject.

For admission eligibility, community and junior colleges, four-year colleges, and universities often require applicants to complete eighteen to twenty-two units of acceptable high school work. Students considering laboratory science as a career should *not* be enrolled in commercial, vocational, or nonacademic programs within high schools. Enrollment in college preparatory high school curriculums will enhance admission requirements to most institutions of higher education.

It is essential that the subject of English be included during each of the four years spent in high school. The ability to read, write, and speak intelligently is increasingly important in health care. Future laboratory science students must have a strong foundation in science; they are urged to include the basic sciences of chemistry, biology, and physics in a high school program. At least two courses in mathematics should be completed, and a student would do well to study the highest level math course consistent with individual ability. As the world grows smaller, knowledge of a foreign language is becoming increasingly important, and two to four units of a language would be helpful.

Completion of English, the sciences, and mathematics as described will yield a minimum of nine of the units needed for collegiate admission. Remaining units may be drawn from courses in social studies, history, and electives. A course in computer science could be considered as one of the elective courses.

What other elective subjects might a high school student select during the secondary school years? Programs in art and music will stimulate an interest in the beauty of sight and sound. A variety of elective courses is enriching; and the better informed one becomes, the better will be future personal decisions. Subjects such as social sciences, history, and philosophy provide some insights into human conduct and principles of being.

A typical high school curriculum that will enhance the chances of one completing a baccalaureate program in laboratory science, includes the following courses:

Courses	Units
English	4
Mathematics	2
Biology	1
Chemistry	1
Physics	1
Foreign Language	2–4
Social Studies	2
Electives	6–8
Total	19–23

A minimum grade point average of 3.0 (B) should be maintained in high school to be successful in a college or university laboratory science program.

B.S. Program in Clinical Laboratory Science/ Medical Technology

The curriculum for becoming a laboratory scientist will vary from institution to institution. However, key courses in college that usually do not change include those in inorganic and organic chemistry and biology.

For the B.S. degree, two sample laboratory science curricula are seen below: one from the University of Minnesota (curriculum A), which is an integrated program and uses the quarter system (eleven weeks = one quarter); the other (curriculum B) is from a 3 + 1 program, using the semester system (sixteen weeks = one semester).

Curriculum A: Clinical Laboratory Science

(Integrated program: suggested curriculum sequence using a quarter system; numbers of credits are in parentheses.)

Fall	Winter	Spring	Summer
Year One			
General Chemistry (5) English Composition (5) Math (5) CLS Orientation (1)	General Chemistry (5) Elective (4–5) Elective (4–5)	General Biology (5) Elective (4–5) Elective (4–5)	
Year Two			
Genetics (4–5) Physics (5) Elective (4–5)	Organic Chemistry (5–6) Physics (5) Elective (4–5)	Organic Chemistry (5–6) Anatomy (5) Elective (4–5)	
Year Three			
Biochemistry (4) Microbiology (4) Elective (4)	Biochemistry (4) Physiology (5) Writing in Science (5)	Math (5) or Statistics (4–5) Pathology (5) Elective (4)	
Year Four			
Intro to Lab Science (2) Chemistry I (4) Hematology I (3) Virology, Mycology, Parasitology (3) Elective (4–5)	Chemistry II (4) Intro to Clinical Microbiology (5) Hemostasis/Instrumentation (3) Management/Education (1)	Chemistry III (4) Immunohematology, Immunology (5) Hematology, Morphology (4)	Clinical Rotations 23 weeks (16–18) (summer and fall)

Total credits needed to graduate: 180 quarter credits

Curriculum B: Clinical Laboratory Science

(3+1 program: suggested curriculum sequence using a semester system; numbers of credits are in parentheses.)

Fall Semester	Spring Semester
Year One	
General Chemistry (4)	General Chemistry (4)
English Composition (4)	Anatomy (4)
General Biology (4)	Electives (7–8)
Mathematics (4)	
Year Two	
Organic Chemistry (5)	Physiology (5)
Physics (5)	Instrumentation (5)
Elective (4–5)	Elective (4–5)
Year Three	
Biochemistry (5)	Immunology (4)
General Microbiology (5)	Computer Science (4)
Histology or Statistics (4–5)	Genetics (4)
	Elective (4)
Year Four	

Clinical rotations (30 credits) are achieved through an accredited hospital program, 50–52 weeks in length. They include hematology, coagulation, microbiology, chemistry, urinalysis, immunohematology, serology, management, and education; some electives such as virology, cytogenetics, research, etc., also are included.

Total credits needed to graduate: 120 semester credits

One may switch from a quarter to semester system (or vice versa) easily. To convert credits from the quarter to semester system, divide the number of quarter credits by two-thirds. Therefore, a quarter course of six credits is equivalent to a semester course of four credits. To convert semester credits to quarter credits, multiply the number of semester credits by one and one-half. Therefore, a two-credit semester course is equivalent to a three-credit quarter course.

It can be seen in curriculum A that students have preclinical courses (year four, fall, winter, spring quarters) prior to their clinical experiences in hospital laboratories. The actual length of time spent in rotations in these hospital laboratories is therefore shortened to twenty-three weeks. In curriculum B, all of the laboratory science professional courses are taught in year four in an accredited hospital program. Total length is fifty to fifty-two weeks.

In some programs, especially those in California, one may need to complete a baccalaureate degree prior to entering a one-year (fifty-week) professional program.

Students interested in laboratory science/medical technology are urged to consult with high school and college advisors who are well-informed about various health science curricula, especially math and science prerequisites. If one switches majors while in college, completion of prerequisite course work also can be accomplished during evening or summer school sessions. A prospective student should check periodically with the director of the professional program he/she is interested in attending to find out whether changes in the curriculum have been made. Accredited program listings can be obtained by writing to the National Accrediting Agency for Clinical Laboratory Sciences, 8410 West Bryn Mawr Avenue, Suite 670, Chicago, IL 60631.

To gain entrance to the professional program in laboratory science/ medical technology (for example, years three or four of curriculum

A or year four of curriculum B), one usually needs a collegiate grade point average (GPA) of close to 3.0 or better (A = 4.0). Some programs may accept a minimum grade point average of 2.5. Admission is usually determined by overall GPA and GPA in prerequisite (science and mathematics) courses. Other factors that may be used by an admissions committee include letters of recommendation, an interview, standardized test scores, and knowledge of the field as evidenced by a written essay or previous laboratory experience. Usually grade point average is considered as the primary determinant for admission.

The Professional Program

Students in laboratory science are expected to become competent professionals. To do so, they are provided with instruction in chemistry/urinalysis; microbiology; blood banking, including immunology/serology; and hematology/coagulation. Often student laboratories are used to provide introductory exercises. Other instruction makes use of case studies, computer-assisted programs, demonstrations, discussions, and research methodology.

"Clinical rotations" refer to the training period of practical experience (an internship) that a student undertakes in a productive laboratory, which is often located in a hospital. The student is under the supervision of practitioners. This experience is exciting, practical, and rewarding as knowledge and skills learned in the classroom and student laboratories are applied in the real world. During clinical rotations, students also interact with patients and other health care providers. Each day of the clinical rotation adds to the students' self-confidence and moves them closer to becoming real professionals.

Personal Attributes

The thirty-item checklist found earlier in this chapter includes some of the personal characteristics that will enhance one's chances of becoming a successful practitioner who enjoys his or her work.

First, an interest in science is very important. Of all high school courses completed, biology is probably the most important. In fact, many professionals believe that an interest and success in biology is more important than an interest and success in chemistry, physics, or mathematics. Thus, one who is interested in biologic processes as well as medical phenomena will be well suited for this profession.

Second, one must have the highest personal integrity. Accurate laboratory information is crucial to the health and well-being of individuals; thus the mislabeling of tubes or specimens, careless work, or reporting erroneous results cannot—and will not—be tolerated. Professionals and students must be able to say, "I made a mistake," and go about correcting it before it can adversely affect a patient.

Third, one must be a good student—intelligent, hardworking, motivated; one who does not put off studying. As in medicine, those in laboratory science want "the brightest and the best," and therefore, achieving a good grade point average is important.

Fourth, one should have good manual dexterity—the ability to manipulate small tubes or microtiter plates, reagents, microscopes, and instruments such as balances or computers in a skillful manner. Usually one's manual dexterity will improve with experience and confidence, but if one cannot handle syringes, pipettes, or delicate instruments skillfully, success in laboratory science may be limited.

Fifth, one should be able to prioritize—to attend to matters that require immediate action, and to be able to decide upon other concerns that can be carried out later and in what order. Patient care is not predictable; often one can receive three STAT (emergency) requests simultaneously. Thus, the laboratorian who can sort out the importance of each and complete the work accurately and in a timely fashion is one of the most valued members of the health care team.

Similar to the ability to prioritize is the ability to work under stress—a person who is "turned on" by the immediacy of a STAT situation, who can remain calm and productive when physicians and nurses are being demanding, and who can communicate with others when they are less than courteous will find laboratory science exciting, meaningful, and very rewarding.

A person who is considering this profession also should be able to plan and carry out tasks with very little supervision. Laboratorians are known for their sense of independence—of being able to analyze a problem or demanding situation and, on their own, go about finishing what needs to be completed. Coupled with many of these attributes is an enjoyment of problem solving. If a person gains a sense of satisfaction in "fixing things," he or she will be much sought after in the laboratory; if able to troubleshoot various instruments, this person will be extremely valued.

Finally, when one considers that, for example, a ten-year span of work involves twenty thousand hours of employment, (usually two thousand hours each year) it is essential that the person interested in laboratory science understand the field, the course work, and personal characteristics required to complete a program, as well as the opportunities available upon graduation. Thus the inquisitive student who tours two or three laboratories, talks to a number of professionals, and visits several accredited educational programs will have an advantage over one who is somewhat interested but not as assertive.

One should note, however, that many laboratory professionals have started school in other majors, such as biology, microbiology, or chemistry. Once they have become knowledgeable about laboratory science, they then switch to it. That, too, is very acceptable, because most people find their career niche not in the first year of school, but later on.

The checklist provides information on other characteristics that are important for success in the profession: a desire to help others, to have a sense of accomplishment for work done well, to be curious, to enjoy learning new things, to enjoy using cutting-edge technologies, to be motivated, and to be able to follow through on projects undertaken.

The potential laboratory science student should understand the hands-on nature of laboratory work. Volunteering to assist in a laboratory will help one gain knowledge of the field, as well as the atmosphere in which it is practiced. It is also important for a student to understand the varied settings, as well as the positive and negative aspects of working in these settings. Finally, one should obtain figures on salaries and benefits—which vary by city, area, region, and setting (such as research versus hospital setting)—so as to understand the financial rewards when one becomes a laboratory professional.

From the above, one might conclude that the laboratory science profession demands intelligent, trustworthy, and caring individuals. This is true, because as health care providers, laboratorians can be nothing less.

Listed next are one graduate's ten rules for survival as a student enrolled in a clinical laboratory science program. These rules reinforce the necessity for character traits of honesty, integrity, and fair-mindedness.

Ten Rules for Survival in Laboratory Science Education

Written by Janice L. Putnam, B.S., a graduate of the University of Minnesota.

1. **Be honest with yourself.** The career you have chosen is one that requires personal integrity and absolute honesty. As a professional, you will be part of a patient care team. It will be your responsibility to perform accurate laboratory tests and interpret the results carefully, so that physicians and other health care workers can determine an appropriate course of patient treatment. If honest work is your policy while in school, it will carry over into your work as a practicing laboratorian. Cheating in school is, of course, dishonest, and may be grounds for dismissal. However, in this field, cheating is much more serious, because it will be harmful to the well-being of a patient. Make a commitment to give the same quality service to patients that you would expect to receive if you were a patient.

2. **Practice respect for your fellow classmates.** You and your classmates are pursuing a mutual goal—graduation in this profession. Along the way, you will spend numerous hours together in lectures, in laboratories, between classes, and in social events. Some of you will become close friends. Others will not share the same closeness.

Every person, however, is unique, and differences among students should be respected. However competition, jealousy, or personal conflicts benefit no one. As a professional, you will have contact with people from varied backgrounds and personalities. If you learn to respect the differences among your classmates, you will be more kind, gentle, and caring of both the patients and other health care providers you will work with as a professional.

3. **Never hesitate to ask for help from your instructors.** The information presented in lectures and practiced in the laboratory is sometimes intense. It may be difficult to comprehend the details, even when reviewing lecture notes and laboratory exercises after class. If you do not understand the material presented, make an appointment to see the instructor. No question is too trivial, and most instructors will gladly take the time to help you comprehend the many aspects of laboratory science.

4. **Budget your time wisely.** The high cost of a college education leaves most students with no choice but to work, in addition to attending classes and studying. Wise utilization of each day is important for successful completion of a program. If outside work is a financial necessity, try to find a job with some flexibility, so that as class schedules change, you can adjust a work schedule accordingly. Attending classes, finishing assigned homework, and studying should be your primary priority. Although it is important to be financially secure, do not allow outside employment to jeopardize your ultimate goal.

5. **Take care of your health.** The demands of college and professional course work can be exhausting. It is impor-

tant to take care of your health in order to be able to
function at the fullest capacity. A healthy diet, drinking
plenty of water, regular exercise, and adequate rest will
keep you alert and energetic enough to meet the challenges of a laboratory science program.

6. **View new information with a questioning mind.** A laboratory professional is a scientist. A scientist who is learning new information should want to know not only what
it means, but also how it came about and how it can be
expanded upon. As a student, you will be presented with
new material every day. Rather than just memorizing the
facts for an exam, question what you have learned. Dis-
cuss it with fellow students and with your instructors.
Expand upon it. Ultimately, success and personal satisfaction in your career will come about when you learn to
think as a scientist.

7. **Listen to upperclass students, but use your own best
judgment.** Whether you choose to accept upperclassmen's
words as "sacred" should be determined by your own
experiences. An unpleasant experience or encounter for
one student is hardly reason for another student to form
prejudices. Enter every class and meet every new instructor with an open mind. Then, based on your own experiences, decide to agree or disagree with the opinions of
upperclass students.

8. **Never stop learning.** This is an evolving profession with
changing methods, better technologies, and increasing
responsibilities. It is imperative that as a student, and then
as a graduate, you continue to learn so as to progress further in the profession. Continuing education may be the

farthest thought from your mind while an undergraduate. However, think ahead toward directions that will enhance your future as a professional.

9. **Take time for fun.** The enjoyment of extracurricular activities is essential for everyone's mental and physical health. Although it is important to put forth a best effort as a student, it is impossible to learn every detail. You will need to take a break. Go to a movie, have dinner with a friend, engage in a hobby or sports activity that is enjoyable, or sit back and watch TV. Relax when the need arises. You will then be better able to enjoy learning.

10. **Act as a professional.** These rules are guides toward becoming a professional. Integrate them into your life. Do *not* ignore laboratory test results that are out of the reference range or do not make sense. Learn how to resolve these and other problems. Keep up to date on the latest advances in diagnostic medicine. Practice the knowledge and skills you have acquired in order to ensure quality patient care. Always act as a professional, which includes keeping yourself well-groomed, well-mannered, and able to get along with others.

These rules represent one student's imperatives to success in school and the profession. They also represent very sound guidelines to success in life.

Applying to a Laboratory Science Program

Once you have decided on a specific program in laboratory science, apply to that program and perhaps two or three others as well. The application means completing a specified form, submitting a transcript, and often providing letters of recommendation. It is important that you fill in all forms neatly and completely, since these are the first pieces of information that members of an admissions committee will see and make judgments upon.

Most applications require submission of an application fee; be sure to include a check or money order in the correct amount and made payable to the institution. (Some organizations hold the application and will not act on it until the check is in receipt.) Follow these common sense directions: make the check payable to the institution's name (not to the name of the admissions officer); be sure the amount of the check equals the application fee; mail the check together with the application in the same envelope; and make certain your account has sufficient funds to cover the check.

Once an admissions committee has received all materials, you may be invited for an interview. This provides the opportunity to visit the school and the laboratory directly. (Even if an interview is not required, visit a program prior to making a commitment.) The interview, although considered an evaluation tool by some, is an instrument of communication that permits direct transmission of information. Dress neatly for the interview, be as poised and confident as you can, and answer all questions truthfully.

In summary, evaluation tools available to an admissions committee include: transcripts, test scores, letters of recommendation, and sometimes interviews. Without question, the transcript is the most important and reliable source of information about an applicant. To an admissions committee, the transcript represents a totality of grades earned by one student over a period of time and from many instructors. Thus it will be used as the primary resource to evaluate your potential.

Once you are accepted into a program, write the program director promptly about your intent to attend. Thereafter, the program director will provide information about starting dates and orientation.

Educational Finances Required

The cost of a baccalaureate education in clinical laboratory science is similar to that in nursing or occupational therapy. Often the first two-to-three preprofessional years are taken in a collegiate setting. In public institutions, tuition may range from $3,000 to $8,000 per year. In private colleges and universities, tuition is much the same as that for other science majors and may cost up to $30,000 per year.

Tuition for the professional component (one to two years) of laboratory sciences education is variable and may be the same as during the preprofessional period. During the professional component, tuition may increase due to the expense of offering laboratory courses.

A variety of scholarships are available to students, especially once they are in the professional program. Scholarships are provided by the American Society for Clinical Laboratory Science (ASCLS) and its state societies, as well as other organizations, such as the American Society of Clinical Pathologists. Loans and grants may be acquired, too; check with the financial aid office of the college or university that you will be attending. You can also research possible scholarships at your local library and on the Internet.

Licensure/Certification

Unlike physicians, nurses, pharmacists, and dentists, who enter their professions via *licensure,* most laboratory professionals enter their fields via *certification*. An explanation of each kind of credential is needed. The first credential (licensure) is required by law; the second (certification) is voluntary but strongly recommended and often required by employers. The purpose of each kind of credential is that of a gatekeeper, that is, to prevent incompetent persons from practicing. Licensure and certification are instituted to help protect the public health, safety, and welfare.

Dentists, nurses, pharmacists, and physicians are usually licensed to practice in the state in which they provide their services. Licensure is the process by which a government or agency grants permission to persons meeting predetermined qualifications to engage in a specific occupation. Usually these predetermined qualifications include completion of a professional program and passing of a state licensure examination. If one is not licensed, he or she cannot legally practice in that state.

In laboratory science, licensure is *not* the primary mode of gatekeeping, except in several states. Personnel licensure exists in Florida, Georgia, Hawaii, Louisiana, Montana, Nevada, New York, North Dakota, Puerto Rico, Rhode Island, Tennessee, and West Virginia but may take the form of a license being granted for successfully passing a national certification examination. California has begun to rely more on national exams, although at the time of this writing the state-developed examination is required for the clinical laboratory scientist/medical technologist level practitioner.

In laboratory science most graduates take certification examinations. Certification is the process by which a nongovernmental agency or association grants recognition to an individual who has met predetermined qualifications—usually passing a certification examination—specified by that agency or association. Certification is voluntary; one does not legally need a certificate to practice.

However, most graduates of laboratory science programs take certification examinations, since employers strongly recommend that employees hold a certificate.

Certification in laboratory science is complex and confusing since there have been multiple agencies involved in providing certification examinations. Table 7 depicts the myriad accreditation agencies in this field. These agencies may certify generalists such as clinical laboratory scientists, or they may certify specialists such as clinical chemists. Some are more highly regarded than others. Thus students should know which employing organizations recognize and expect certain credentials. A brief review of major agencies certifying generalists is provided below.

Table 7 List of Laboratory Certifications and the Agencies Sponsoring Each

Organization	Certification (full title)	Certification (abbreviation)
	Generalist	
American Association of Bioanalysts (AAB)	Medical Technologist	MT (AAB)
	Laboratory Technician	MLT (AAB)
National Credentialing Agency for Laboratory Personnel	Clinical Laboratory Scientist	CLS (NCA)
	Clinical Laboratory Technician	CLT (NCA)
Board of Registry of the American Society of Clinical Pathologists	Medical Technologist	MT (ASCP)
	Medical Laboratory Technician	MLT (ASCP)
American Medical Technologists	Medical Technologist	MT (AMT)
	Medical Laboratory Technician	MLT (AMT)
American Association of Bioanalysts	Registered Medical Technologist	MT (AAB)
	Registered Medical Laboratory Technician	MLT (AAB)
Health, Education and Welfare	Clinical Laboratory Technologist	CLT (HEW)

Table 7 Continued

Organization	Certification (full title)	Certification (abbreviation)
Management (Generalist)		
National Credentialing Agency for Laboratory Personnel	Clinical Laboratory Supervisor Clinical Laboratory Director	CLSup (NCA) CLDir (NCA)
Board of Registry (ASCP)	Diplomate in Laboratory Management	DLM (ASCP)
American Association of Bioanalysts	Bioanalyst Laboratory Manager Bioanalyst Laboratory Supervisor	BLM BLS
American Board of Bioanalysis	Bioanalyst Laboratory Director Bioanalyst Clinical Laboratory Director	BLD BCLD
American Medical Technologists Institute of Certified Professional Managers	Certified Laboratory Manager	CLM (AMT)
Blood Banking		
Board of Registry (ASCP)	Technologist in Blood Banking Specialist in Blood Banking	BB (ASCP) SBB (ASCP)
Chemistry		
American Board of Bioanalysts	Clinical Laboratory Director	CLD
American Board of Clinical Chemistry	Diplomate in Clinical Chemistry Diplomate in Toxicology	DABCC DABCC
Board of Registry (ASCP)	Technologist in Chemistry Specialist in Chemistry	C (ASCP) SC (ASCP)
National Credentialing Agency for Laboratory Personnel (NCA)	Clinical Laboratory Scientist	CLS (C)
National Registry in Clinical Chemistry	Clinical Chemistry Technologist Clinical Chemist Toxicological Chemist	CCT (NRCC) CC (NRCC) TC (NRCC)

Table 7 Continued

Organization	Certification (full title)	Certification (abbreviation)
	Cytogenetics	
National Credentialing Agency for Laboratory Personnel (NCA)	Clinical Laboratory Specialist in Cytogenetics	CLSpCG (NCA)
	Cytology	
Board of Registry (ASCP)	Cytotechnologist	CT (ASCP)
	Specialist in Cytotechnology	SCT (ASCP)
International Academy of Cytology	Cytotechnologist	CT (IAC)
	Hemapheresis	
Board of Registry (ASCP)	Hemapheresis Practitioner	HP (ASCP)
	Hematology	
National Credentialing Agency for Laboratory Personnel	Clinical Laboratory Specialist in Hematology	CLSp (H) (NCA)
Board of Registry (ASCP)	Technologist in Hematology	H (ASCP)
	Specialist in Hematology	SH (ASCP)
	Histology	
Board of Registry (ASCP)	Histologic Technician	HT (ASCP)
	Histotechnologist	HTL (ASCP)
	Immunology	
American Society for Microbiology American Academy of Microbiology	Diplomate	D (ABMLI)

Table 7 Continued

Organization	Certification (full title)	Certification (abbreviation)
Immunology (Continued)		
National Credentialing Agency for Laboratory Personnel (NCA)	Clinical Laboratory Scientist (Immunohematology)	CLS (I)
National Credentialing Agency for Laboratory Personnel (NCA)	Clinical Laboratory Scientist (Microbiology)	CLS (M)
American Board of Medical Laboratory Immunology		
Board of Registry (ASCP)	Technologist in Immunology Specialist in Immunology	I (ASCP) SI (ASCP)
Microbiology		
American Society for Microbiology American Academy of Microbiology American Board of Medical Microbiology	Diplomate	D (ABMM)
National Registry of Microbiologists	Specialist Microbiologist Registered Microbiologist	SM (NRM) RM (NRM)
Board of Registry (ASCP)	Technologist in Microbiology Specialist in Microbiology	M (ASCP) SM (ASCP)
National Credentialing Agency for Laboratory Personnel (NCA)	Clinical Laboratory Scientist (Hematology)	CLS (H)
Molecular Biology		
National Credentialing Agency for Laboratory Personnel (NCA)	Specialist in Molecular Biology	CLSp (MB)

Table 7 Continued

Organization	Certification (full title)	Certification (abbreviation)
	Phlebotomy	
National Credentialing Agency for Laboratory Personnel	Clinical Laboratory Phlebotomist	CLPlb (NCA)
Board of Registry (ASCP)	Phlebotomy Technician	PBT (ASCP)
American Society of Phlebotomy Technicians	Certified Phlebotomy Technician	CPT (ASPT)
International Academy of Phlebotomy Science	Phlebotomist	CPT (IAPS)
National Phlebotomy Association	Phlebotomy Technologist	CPT (NPA)
	Radiology	
American Registry of Radiologic Technologists	Registered Nuclear Medicine Technologist	RT (N) (ARRT)
Nuclear Medicine Technology Certification Board	Nuclear Medicine Technologist	CNMT

Adapted and updated from *Medical Laboratory Observer.*

Board of Registry of the American Society of Clinical Pathologists (ASCP)

In 1928 the American Society of Clinical Pathologists (ASCP) established the Registry of Technicians to register individuals who met certain requirements in training and education. The first certificates that were awarded required graduation from high school or a diploma from a school of nursing and one year of training. In 1933 applicants were required to pass an essay examination and an oral and practical (hands-on) examination before certification was granted. In 1934 educational requirements were increased to two years of college including science courses and one year of clinical training. Following is the actual examination given in 1933.

Registry Examination, October 1933

1. Name five divisions of the clinical laboratory in well organized work. In which divisions or division of the clinical laboratory has the applicant had the most training? Outline the nature of the practical training. In what division has the applicant had little or no training?
2. Define: meniscus, artifact, bacterial antigen, pyogenic, autolysis, hemolytic.
3. Define: metastasis, aspiration, Negri bodies, pyrexia.
4. Define: pediatrics, otology, neurology, psychiatry, orthopedics, pathology, gynecology, radiography, gastroenterology, ophthalmology.
5. Define: cylindroid, hypychlorhydria, physiological leukocytosis, hemoglobinuria, symbiosis.

Clinical
1. Define: endotoxin, chromogenic, anaerobic, attenuation symbiosis.
2. Name six organisms representing normal respiratory flora.

Hematology
1. Name the procedures included in the routine examination of the blood.
2. Distinguish by [drawing]: squamous epithelial cell, normal erythrocyte, normal lymphocyte, blood platelet, and pus cell.

Urinalysis
1. Name seven factors which should be included in the routine examination of the urine.

Serology
1. Name serological tests in the clinical diagnosis of syphilis, undulant fever, typhoid, and paratyphoid.

Tissue Technic
1. What is the most satisfactory fixing fluid for tissues?

The 2 + 1 (2 years college + 1 year training) pattern continued until 1962, when these requirements were replaced by a baccalaureate degree. The late 1960s and 1970s saw the rise of 2 + 2 baccalaureate programs, primarily in large colleges, universities, and medical centers, in addition to traditional 3 + 1 programs.

In 1963 the Board of Registry of the ASCP began providing certification examinations for laboratory technicians. The Board of Registry has also certified individuals other than generalists: cytotechnologists, histotechnologists, histologic technicians, and phlebotomists; technologists in chemistry, cytotechnology, hematology, immunology, microbiology, and nuclear medicine, as well as specialists in blood banking, chemistry, cytotechnology, hemapheresis, hematology, immunology, and microbiology.

National Credentialing Agency for Laboratory Personnel (NCA)

In 1977 the American Society for Medical Technology helped to establish a new certification agency independent of control by any professional association. Prior to that time, the Board of Registry, under the auspices of the ASCP (a pathologist group), controlled the certification of the majority of laboratory personnel. Moreover, Board of Registry certificants had no voting rights under the ASCP. Many laboratory professionals chafed under these arrangements and initiated the National Credentialing Agency (NCA).

In 1978 NCA offered its first examinations for two generalist categories: the category of clinical laboratory scientist (CLS) and that of clinical laboratory technician (CLT). Other NCA examinations are now available, including those in management (for the clinical laboratory supervisor and clinical laboratory director), as well as in specialty areas such as cytogenetics, phlebotomy, and hematology.

Many laboratory personnel believe that NCA best represents their interests as the preferred certifying body. NCA has a sound reputation, primarily because of the excellence of its examinations, which are based on competence statements of actual practice in the laboratory.

Moreover, NCA seeks *recertification* of its certificants—either through completion of continuing education credits or through retesting. NCA is thus committed to continuing competence, not just initial certification. The NCA is known, therefore, for its excellent and comprehensive examinations, as well as for certificants' commitment to providing evidence of ongoing competence.

Other Agencies

Other agencies have provided certification examinations for laboratory generalists:

American Medical Technologists (AMT)

In 1939 a group of laboratory personnel founded AMT, a certification agency used mainly by graduates of proprietary schools. In addition, AMT approved laboratory education programs through the Accrediting Bureau of Health Education Schools. AMT certification requirements focus on technical training and work experience. Previously members of AMT tended to be graduates of one- or two-year proprietary schools who first qualified for the technician category and then, with work experience and passing of the AMT technologist's examination, gained medical technologist (MT) status.

American Association of Bioanalysts (AAB) formerly the International Society for Clinical Laboratory Technology (ISCLT)

Founded as a splinter group of AMT, ISCLT was a professional society of laboratory personnel with a membership composed primarily of persons trained on the job (OJTs). ISCLT began providing a certification examination in 1962 through its credentialing commission; its efforts have been directed to the registered medical technologist (RMT) and registered laboratory technician (RLT) categories. ISCLT examinations are available to persons who have had experience in the laboratory and who are sponsored by a supervisor.

Department of Health, Education and Welfare (HEW)

To further complicate certification efforts, the federal government began providing proficiency examinations for supportive-level personnel in 1975. The intent of these examinations was to ensure that those independent laboratories that performed testing for Medicare patients had sufficient "properly qualified technical personnel." At that time, many independent laboratories employed numerous supportive-level personnel but fewer persons holding degrees. Since Medicare requirements for reimbursement were quite stringent—for example, that a supervisor be in attendance while supportive-level personnel were working—many independent laboratories, and some hospital laboratories as well, did not meet Medicare standards.

The Department of Health, Education and Welfare—now Health and Human Services (HHS)—tried to "upgrade" the status of workers employed through examination rather than "downgrade" its original standards. Approximately fifty thousand laboratorians took the HEW examinations in an attempt to gain status and perhaps to prepare for further governmental regulations. Approximately one-half passed the exams and were certified by HEW as clinical laboratory technologists or cytotechnologists. (Contact the Department of Health and Human Services in Washington, D.C., for information on the status of the current HHS proficiency test for laboratory personnel.)

Other Certification Agencies

In addition to these agencies that have certified generalist laboratory personnel, there also exist a number of organizations that credential laboratory specialists. These organizations include the American Board of Bioanalysts, American Board of Clinical Chemistry, National Registry in Clinical Chemistry, International Academy of Cytology, American Society for Microbiology, American Society of Phlebotomy Technicians, International Academy of Phlebotomy Science, National Phlebotomy Association, American Registry of Radiologic Technologists, and Nuclear Medicine Technology Certification Board. Altogether at least fifteen different groups have provided or are providing certification examinations for various personnel in clinical laboratories.

The multiplicity of agencies and designations used have contributed to some of the confusion—especially for the public—

regarding credentialed laboratorians. It also has prevented a united front in terms of the politics that concern laboratory personnel. Nonetheless, experienced employers know which credentials are meritorious and indicate competence of laboratorians.

Graduate Programs

Clinical laboratory scientists are very well suited to enroll in graduate programs, both at the master's and doctoral levels. Their backgrounds suit them well for such advanced degrees. Examples of programs for which baccalaureate-level graduates may enroll include, but are not limited to, the following:

Anatomy
Bacteriology
Biochemistry
Biomedical engineering
Biometry
Business administration
Cell biology
Clinical chemistry
Clinical laboratory
  science
Computer and
  information systems
Education
Environmental health
Epidemiology
Genetics
Health informatics

Hematology
Hemostasis
History of medicine
Immunohematology
Immunology
Laboratory medicine
Management
Medical technology
Microbial
  engineering
Microbiology
Molecular diagnostics
Pathology (pathobiology)
Pharmacology
Physiology
Public health
Virology

Students may find areas of interest within other programs whose designated names may not always indicate graduate-level opportunities. Thus, a "specialization" in hematology may be found within a "department" such as anatomy. An "immunology" concentration might well be seen in pathobiology, or an "epidemiology" emphasis may be within a school of public health.

Undergraduate (baccalaureate level) students who wish to obtain an advanced degree should take the Graduate Record Examination (GRE) close to the time of graduation, when course work is still very familiar. For those whose grade point average is below a 3.0 (A = 4.0), completion of additional courses is strongly advised because that GPA (B average) is a minimum for many graduate programs.

The American Society for Clinical Laboratory Science has published a *Directory of Graduate Programs for Clinical Laboratory Practitioners*, which includes information on U.S. master's- and doctoral-level programs in clinical laboratory science. Updated information can be found at the ASCLS website.

Finally, *Peterson's Guides* (found in most medical libraries) list the programs and schools that offer advanced degrees. Take some time to do a little research so you can decide whether an investment in clinical laboratory science will be satisfying and meaningful.

6

ISSUES FOR THE PROFESSION AND THE PRACTITIONER

EVERY PROFESSION CHANGES and evolves, or it dies. Changes are now being experienced by all of the health professions and include moving from little regulation by state or federal governments to considerable regulation by each; changes in how the profession credentials its practitioners; and changes that have to do with how one profession comes to deal with another to deliver health care and to be reimbursed for it. Competition—who can compete with whom to do what and for what charge—is often determined by what are known as "scope-of-practice" definitions. These are generally contained in state or federal laws, such as state practice or licensure acts, or federal laws concerned with Medicare or Medicaid.

All health care providers are experiencing tremendous change as well. Specialty physicians such as anesthesiologists are being replaced by generalist practitioners such as family practice physicians. Nurse practitioners are taking a primary role in screening and referring patients, as well as in prescribing medications. Some professions such as those in physical therapy have by state law an independent practice that does not require physician referral and is reimbursed directly for services provided.

Health care institutions themselves are undergoing change. Managed care, emphasizing wellness and disease prevention is replacing the traditional hospital as the main site for providing health services. Surgeries are being performed in ambulatory care settings. More and more laboratories are located outside of traditional hospitals and clinics. And, the reimbursement for all services is changing as well.

Thus, clinical laboratory science is going through changes today in relation to medicine and, to a lesser extent, to nursing and to other allied health professions. Such changes are taking the forms of issues that must be resolved, first within each profession through the process of building consensus, and then among the professions involved.

Political issues are just as important for the professional to master and affect as are the scientific, technical, and valuing principles underlying his or her field. Politics have an enormous influence on what professionals do every day; whether they will be able to expand their roles and duties as new technologies and new roles broaden their competence; and how much satisfaction and money they will derive from their profession.

This chapter focuses on a few of the main issues with which today's clinical laboratory professionals are grappling. They include: professional independence, health care cost containment and laboratory reimbursement, and potential changes in practice patterns.

The Struggle for Professional Independence

One of the more intriguing aspects concerning contemporary health care is the struggle being waged by the allied health professions, including clinical laboratory science, for independence from medicine. Like nursing, many of the allied health professions began as helping occupations, and early on they were subordinate to medicine. Practitioners performed routine tasks as requested by doctors.

However, changes in science, technology, and professional expertise, coupled with insights into health care needs and capabilities and, lately, unprecedented pressures on the health care delivery system, have combined to advance these former "helping occupations" to their status today as professions, or near-professions. With that step has come laboratory science practitioners' understandable desire to practice to the full extent of their professional abilities. As their competence in laboratory science has expanded, however, it has inevitably brought practitioners from an earlier subordinate position to collegial status. Results have included tensions over professional territory and compensation.

The issues at stake are basically how the two fields, pathology and clinical laboratory science, will interact in the future, and whether clinical laboratory science will gain autonomy from pathology. The struggle began over sixty years ago; just how far clinical laboratory science has come can be seen in a brief history of the field and in how its statements, or codes, of professional ethics have evolved.

A Brief History of Clinical Laboratory Science

M. Ruth Williams, an early historian of the profession, has provided several possibilities for how clinical laboratory science began. One possibility, which she attributes to Vivian Herrick, a medical technologist writing in 1937 in the *American Journal of Medical Technology*, is that the profession can trace its beginnings to 1550 B.C., when certain intestinal parasites were mentioned in writing. Another is that in the fourteenth century, in Bologna, Italy, a young woman named Alessandra Giliani served as the first laboratorian. She was employed, we are told, by a physician at the University of Bologna in "performing certain tasks which would now be considered those of the technologist." She eventually died from a laboratory-acquired infection.

Others, however, prefer to date the profession much later, in the 1600s. According to Herrick, "Malpighi (1628–1694) is described as the greatest of the early microscopists and his work in embryology and anatomy definitely marks him as the founder of pathology." Others date the founding of laboratory science "with Anton van Leeuwenhoeck's description of red blood cells (1674), protozoa and bacteria (1677)."

Some prefer an even later date, linking the profession's origins to Pasteur and Koch and their advances in bacteriology (1857 and 1876, respectively), or to Virchow who specialized in cellular physiology and who is credited with having founded the Archives of Pathology in Berlin, in 1847.

Williams writes that the first "chemical laboratory" associated with medicine in the United States was founded at the University of Michigan around 1844. A laboratory assistant at that time (later to become a physician and dean of the Michigan College of Medicine) described some of his work:

> I remember with what pride I demonstrated leukemic blood and urine to the class; how I exhibited crystals of tyrosin and leucin in the urine in a case of cancer of the liver, a rare opportunity indeed; how I showed the presence of urea in the perspiration of a man dying of kidney disease. (Vaughan)

Although some of the procedures Vaughan describes are routine today, he captured an excitement that still is felt when a clinical laboratory professional discovers an important diagnostic clue.

A synopsis of the evolution of major diagnostic events in laboratory science over the last hundred years follows:

The Evolution of Diagnostic Technologies

1900s:
- Wright stain for blood smears
- Wasserman complement fixation test
- hydrogen electrode for blood pH

1910s:
- preparation of vaccines
- microtome (cutting tissue sections)
- Van Slyke apparatus (blood gases)

1920s:
- Folin-Wu method for whole blood sugar
- closed tube hematocrit
- colorimeter

1930s:
- titrimetric methods
- agglutination reaction
- one-stage prothrombin time

1940s:
- precipitation reaction
- immunofluorescence
- Coleman Jr. spectrophotometer®

1950s:
- flame photometry
- indirect fluorescent antibody technique
- "quality control"

1960s:
- blood cell counters
- multichannel chemistry analyzers, e.g., Technicon AutoAnalyzer®
- paper chromatography
- radioimmunoassay

1970s:
- high pressure liquid chromatography
- monoclonal antibody immunoassays
- "closed chemistry" systems, e.g., DuPont aca®

1980s:
- "dry" chemistries, e.g., Kodak Ektachem 400®
- polymerase chain reaction
- flow cytometry

1990s:
- biosensors (chem + computer chip)
- "in vivo" sensors, e.g., for glucose
- nanotechnology

2000s:
- DNA microarrays
- miniaturization in medical diagnostic technologies
- noninvasive, or minimally invasive, technologies (like the watch-style monitor for diabetes)

One of the first official references to laboratory workers is found in the 1900 census which listed 100 technicians, all male, employed in the United States. These were not all medical technicians, but included some dental and industrial workers. The number of technicians had increased to 3,500 by 1920, with 2,000 of these female. . . . [By] 1922, 3,035 hospitals reported they had clinical laboratories. (Williams)

Following World War I, the demand grew for appropriately trained laboratory technicians. In 1922 the first baccalaureate program in medical technology was founded at the University of Minnesota, to be followed shortly thereafter by another baccalaureate-level program at the University of Tennessee.

In 1928 the American Society of Clinical Pathologists (ASCP), an organization of pathologists who employed technicians, established certain qualifications for technicians and then created a Board of Registry to certify individuals who met its qualifications to practice.

By 1933, however, some technicians recognized the need for their own professional association. With the founding that year of the forerunner of the American Society for Clinical Laboratory Science—then called the American Society of Clinical Laboratory Technicians—the struggle for professional independence had begun. For example, by 1943, Frieda Claussen, the fourth national president of the Society, wrote of the confusion regarding ASCP's Board of Registry being a certifying agency while ASCLT was a professional association of laboratory technologists. In her minutes of the Board of Registry meeting with its Advisory Committee, she noted:

The fact that we have a national organization, the American Society of Medical Technologists, whose membership is composed entirely of technologists registered with the A.S.C.P., seems to have escaped the notice of many registrants, who are not aware that the national organization and the Registry are not one and the same, and who through this lack of understanding have failed to give their support to the A.S.M.T. Without a strong national organization the technologists of America can never hope to hold their own in the solution of any problem. Registration with the "Registry" is not the same as belonging to the American Society of Medical Technologists as the Registry is not a society.

Although clinical laboratory practitioners may work closely with pathologists in the laboratory, clinical laboratory science is not part of the practice of medicine. However, because some pathologists provide clinical laboratory services and because laboratory science has a history closely associated with pathology, some disagree.

Nevertheless, several state attorneys general and the United States Department of Health and Human Services (HHS), in a regulation upheld by the United States Court of Appeals, found that medicine and clinical laboratory science were different professions.

In a 1976 opinion, for instance, the Attorney General for Minnesota, Warren Spannaus, wrote to Arthur W. Poore, Executive Secretary, Minnesota Board of Medical Examiners (Correspondence. January 5, 1976 [303c]):

> You ask . . . substantially the following. . . .
>
> Does the scientific testing and reporting of results of medical laboratories of samples obtained from human beings performed only for and at the request of licensed physicians, constitute the practice of medicine?
>
> We answer your question in the negative.
>
> In our opinion, the function performed by the medical laboratories does not constitute diagnosis. . . . Rather, the labs are engaged in ascertaining observable or quantifiable facts. . . .
>
> This result is consistent with the opinions of Attorneys General of other states dealing with the line between the unauthorized practice of medicine and licensed laboratory testing. . . .

The advent of automated test technologies in the 1950s and the creation of the Medicare and Medicaid programs in the late 1960s, together with the assertions of laboratory professionals in the 1960s, intensified the struggle between pathology and clinical laboratory science.

Automated multichannel test instruments meant that large volumes of samples could be tested quickly, cheaply, and usually reliably. Medicare and Medicaid programs, which were created in 1965 transformed the federal government into a major purchaser of laboratory services for the elderly and the needy, stimulating a huge demand for health care services that has still not been contained. The question of laboratory ownership, direction, and control became a struggle between elements of organized pathology and nonphysician clinical laboratory practitioners; the real issues—professional autonomy and access to compensation for services within one's scope of practice—were often buried beneath unjustified challenges regarding the nonphysician's competence and qualifications to serve in directoral roles.

Three major events contributed to the pathologist versus technologist rift that occurred in the 1960s. First, Janice Higgins, a registered technologist from New Jersey, was denied recertification by the Board of Registry of ASCP. Higgins worked in a bioanalyst laboratory, and she had no pathologist to cosign her recertification form, a requirement at that time. In 1964 Higgins sued the Board of Registry of ASCP because her livelihood was threatened, and in 1968 the Supreme Court of New Jersey ruled in her favor. More than the ruling, the case brought to light that medical technologists' very employment was dependent on pathologists' approval.

Second, in 1966 the Justice Department investigated the College of American Pathologists (CAP) for antitrust action, primarily regarding fee-setting and exclusionary practices. The Justice Department settled with CAP in a cease-and-desist order. However, because ASMT had collaborated with the other pathologist group, ASCP, in accreditation and in certification (the Board of Registry), the Justice Department also cited ASMT for taking a "supine" position in the matters of antitrust as well as credentialing. Members of the Board of Directors of ASMT were astounded that they should be so cited, but their eyes were also opened as to how this affiliation with ASCP was perceived by others.

Third, many members of ASMT were disconcerted with the management of the Board of Registry. Again, Ruth Williams has chronicled the events. She writes:

Throughout the 1960s, ASMT representatives to the Board of Registry believed they were being ignored in matters of policy. A proposed amendment to the ASCP bylaws was interpreted to indicate that the ASCP expected to elect the ASMT representatives to the Board. An attempt was made to settle the dispute before a neutral mediator, and promises were exchanged, but neither side yielded.

The ASCP continued to maintain that the Board of Registry was constituted as, and remained a standing committee of the ASCP. The ASMT continued to express the desire to assume a larger role in decision making in areas affecting medical technology. The breach between the societies widened when ASCP voted a third category of laboratory workers (the medical laboratory technician) without consultation with the members of the Board.

When it became apparent to the officers of the ASMT that no further progress in achieving harmony was possible, the ASMT decided it had no recourse except to refer the disagreements to the court. Hence, in May 1969, suit was filed in the U.S. District Court of the Northern District of Illinois. The complaints, in brief, were:

1. ASCP had attempted to monopolize interstate trade and commerce in commercial medical laboratories in violation of the Sherman Act.
2. The monies collected by the Board of Registry for examinations, renewals of certificates, etc., came from medical technologists. Such monies should not be diverted to uses other than operation of the Registry.
3. ASCP had not granted equal representation to ASMT on the Board of Registry.
4. The ASCP took action to change the composition of the Board of Registry with the exclusion of ASMT. ASMT alleged this constituted a violation of federal antitrust laws, since it was an attempt to achieve complete monopoly in the laboratories.
5. The "affiliate" (but non-voting) membership offered to medical technologists by ASCP threatened to monopolize and control the profession.
6. Because pathologists had the power to fix salaries of medical technologists, this power could be used to coerce them to join ASCP as affiliate members.

ASMT lost the decision in 1971, based not on the substance of the issue, but on legal technicalities. The real issues, including affiliate membership or representation on the Board of Registry, were never debated.

The Board of Directors of ASMT decided against pursuing additional appeals, since negotiations with ASCP resulted in the formation of the National Accrediting Agency for Clinical Laboratory Sciences (NAACLS), a freestanding accreditation agency, in 1973. When the ASMT proposed further discussion with ASCP about control of the Board of Registry in 1974, ASCP refused to consider the matter.

The rift between ASCP and ASMT continued into the 1970s, when ASMT withdrew its representatives to the Board of Registry in 1976 and established the National Certification Agency for Medical Laboratory Personnel (NCA)—now known as the National Credentialing Agency for Laboratory Personnel—independent of a "sponsoring" group.

Why do many laboratorians believe that NCA is so important to the profession, and why might it be important in the future? First, in the very definition of a profession, it is crucial that the profession—not another group—determine how entrance to the practice is achieved. Whether credentialing by certification or licensure, each profession must define its own standards for practice as well as entry to that practice.

Second, to ensure credibility with the public, each profession must establish its standards for demonstrating continued competence. The NCA, through its recertification process (usually via continuing education), verifies to the public that its registrants maintain high standards of practice, even years after initial certification.

Third, unless clinical laboratorians are in control of their own certification or licensure processes, they will be viewed by colleagues in nursing, physical therapy, pharmacy, medicine, and others, as less than equal. Many allied health professionals cannot understand why, with the education and training laboratory scientists hold, they do not take full control of their own destiny.

Fourth, with federal and state governments enacting legislation and ensuing regulations, it is important that these legislators and agency officials respect the profession. To earn that respect, and these persons' attention, laboratory professionals need to demonstrate that they—not a pathologist group—best represent the profession.

The struggle continued throughout the 1980s, especially through laboratorians' support of the Clinical Laboratory Improvements Act (CLIA) of 1988, which was enacted to give all laboratories the same set of standards for testing. Establishing the regulations to accompany this Act were further complicated, and for more than twelve years, often divisive. In the 1980s and 1990s ASCP took few positions on CLIA even though ninety thousand physician office laboratories were unregulated. The main concern of the ASCP involved who was directing the laboratories, e.g., physicians. In contrast, ASMT and its successor, ASCLS, fought for personnel standards, the credentialing of personnel performing tests, and evidence of continued competency. In the 1990s ASCLS and ASCP continued to have different positions regarding government regulations and personnel.

However, due to the support of multiple laboratory organizations, in April of 1995, the National Labor Relations Board (NLRB) officially included medical technologists among its "professional employees" as defined by Section 2(12) of the National Labor Relations Act. This decision was based on the education and training required of technologists, the need for judgment in evaluating test data, and CLIA regulations requiring laboratorians' participation in proficiency testing to ensure the accuracy of their work. The NLRB decision noted that "this congressional concern (CLIA) regarding the skills required of medical technologists underscores the professional nature of their work." The NLRB also compared the educational requirement for laboratorians and registered nurses and stated that the education and certification procedures for technologists were often equal to or greater than those for RNs.

Following are the categories of personnel within the National Labor Relations Board's jurisdiction.

Hospital Employee Categories as Established by the National Labor Relations Board

1. physicians
2. registered nurses
3. other non-MD professionals, e.g., medical technologists (clinical laboratory scientists)
4. technical employees, e.g., medical (clinical) laboratory technicians
5. clerical employees
6. skilled maintenance workers
7. other nonprofessionals
8. security guards

Note: The NLRB defines "professional employees" as those who meet four conjunctive criteria and engage in work that: is predominantly intellectual and varied in character as opposed to routine work; requires consistent exercise of discretion and judgment; is not standardized in relation to a given period of time; and requires knowledge of an advanced type in a field of science or learning customarily acquired by a prolonged course of study.

Professional Ethics

A great deal can be learned about the evolution of a profession from comparing its various codes of ethics in a historical context. Codes of ethics address what members of a profession believe are its defining characteristics, the functions and roles that distinguish them from others, and their duties and responsibilities to society.

In 1928, when the Board of Registry of Laboratory Technicians was formed via a physician group, a code of ethics was submitted that those who were registered would agree to follow. It reads:

> All registered technicians and technologists shall be required to strictly observe the Code of Ethics as defined by the American Society of Clinical Pathologists, namely, that they shall agree to work at all times under the supervision of a qualified physician and shall under no circumstances, on their own initiative, render written or oral diagnoses except insofar as it is self-evident in the report, or advise physicians or others in the treatment of disease, or operate a laboratory independently without the supervision of a qualified physician or clinical pathologist. (Registry of Technicians, ASCP [1928])

For many years, medical technologists followed the Code, established by the ASCP.

In 1955, the American Society of Medical Technology published its first Code of Ethics, based on premises established by the ASCP:

Section 1.   A member of the Society shall at all times work only under the direction and supervision of a pathologist or duly qualified doctor of medicine or specialist in one of the divisions of clinical pathology, such qualifications being determined on the basis of accepted medical ethics.

Section 2.   A member of this Society shall make no diagnosis or interpretations other than those in the reports prepared by him.

Section 3.   A member of this Society shall not advise physicians or others how to treat disease.

Section 4.   A member of this Society shall not train students without supervision of a clinical pathologist.

Section 5. A member of this Society shall not engage in laboratory work independent of qualified supervision (as provided in Section 1) nor shall he operate an independent laboratory.

Section 6. It is ethical to perform laboratory work on a commission basis under contract with a public health, research, or clinical laboratory when such work is done as provided in Section 1 above and when all contractual agreements are approved and signed by the director of the organization contracting for such services.

However, only two years later, in 1957, the ASMT adopted a different Code of Ethics:

Being fully cognizant of my responsibilities in the practice of Medical Technology, I affirm my willingness to discharge my duties with accuracy, thoughtfulness, and care.

Realizing that the knowledge obtained concerning patients in the course of my work must be treated as confidential I hold inviolate the confidence (trust) placed in me by patient and physician.

Recognizing that my integrity and my profession must be pledged to the absolute reliability of my work, I will conduct myself at all times in a manner appropriate to the dignity of my profession.

Forty-five years ago the practice of laboratory science, as perceived by members of its first professional association, was simply a matter of accuracy, confidentiality, reliability, and dignity—all essential behaviors, but behaviors that should characterize any professional. That early code really pertained to a supporting practitioner; it did not address the duties a true profession would expect from and require of its members.

The ASMT Code of Ethics was revised considerably in 1988 and then updated by the ASCLS in 1995. Today it describes a much different professional, this one with clear responsibilities in the laboratory, to the patient, to the profession, and in the community at large.

Code of Ethics of the American Society for Clinical Laboratory Science (1995)

Preamble

The Code of Ethics of the American Society for Clinical Laboratory Science (ASCLS) sets forth the principles and standards by which clinical laboratory professionals practice their profession.

I. Duty to the Patient

Clinical laboratory professionals are accountable for the quality and integrity of the laboratory services they provide. This obligation includes maintaining individual competence in judgment and performance and striving to safeguard the patient from incompetent or illegal practice by others.

Clinical laboratory professionals maintain high standards of practice. They exercise sound judgment in establishing, performing and evaluating laboratory testing.

Clinical laboratory professionals maintain strict confidentiality of patient information and test results. They safeguard the dignity and privacy of patients and provide accurate information to other health care professionals about the services they provide.

II. Duty to Colleagues and the Profession

Clinical laboratory professionals uphold and maintain the dignity and respect of our profession and maintain a reputation of honesty, integrity and reliability. They contribute to the advancement of the profession by improving the body of knowledge, adopting scientific advances that benefit the patient, maintaining high standards of practice and education, and seeking fair socioeconomic working conditions for members of the profession.

Clinical laboratory professionals actively strive to establish cooperative and respectful working relationships with other health professionals with the primary objective of ensuring a high standard of care for the patients they serve.

III. Duty to Society

As practitioners of an autonomous profession, clinical laboratory professionals have the responsibility to contribute from their sphere of professional competence to the general well being of the community.

Clinical laboratory professionals comply with relevant laws and regulations pertaining to the practice of clinical laboratory science and actively seek within the dictates of their consciences, to change those which do not meet the high standards of care and practice to which the profession is committed.

Pledge to the Profession

As a clinical laboratory professional, I strive to:

- Maintain and promote standards of excellence in performing and advancing the art and science of my profession;
- Preserve the dignity and privacy of patients;
- Uphold and maintain the dignity and respect of our profession;
- Seek to establish cooperative and respectful working relationships with other health professionals; and
- Contribute to the general well being of the community.

I shall demonstrate my commitment to these responsibilities throughout my professional life.

(Reprinted with permission of the American Society for Clinical Laboratory Science, © 1997–2001.)

How Law and Regulation Affect the Profession

Today federal, state, and local laws and regulations influence every facet of any health care profession. Some laws and regulations influence who may perform clinical laboratory services; some determine how they shall be paid; others mandate safety precautions to protect the patient and practitioner; and others establish general quality assurance safeguards, to name just a few of the issues.

In fact, a great deal of what takes place every day in the laboratory occurs at least partly because of federal, state, or local governmental requirements. Laboratory practitioners themselves carry out the quality control, record-keeping, hiring, safety, and other requirements of law or regulations not only because these functions represent safe and competent practice, but also because they are responsible for ensuring compliance with such requirements.

Drug testing gives an example of how the federal government affects daily practice in the laboratory. Who performs drug testing; what drugs are involved; what quantities of each (or threshold concentrations) will be detected; and what technical procedures, quality control, security, and confidentiality safeguards are imposed on the specimen collection, handling, and testing process are among the issues addressed in regulations concerning drug testing for military personnel and certain civilian employees, such as airline pilots.

Taken as a whole, federal, state, and local laws and regulations govern the laboratory facility, its personnel, many of its analytic procedures, and its quality assurance practices. Federal laws and regulations also provide civil rights protections and antidiscrimination safeguards for employees; set up procedures for labor disputes; regulate medical devices, blood, and blood products; and influence a great many other aspects of laboratory practice.

More important in some ways, however, federal regulations especially influence the profession, the practitioner, and the public in other ways that are perhaps more profound but not necessarily as evident.

Thus, practicing professionals must have a thorough understanding of the government's role, and prospective students should be aware of the powerful influence exerted by laws and regulations on the profession and the practitioner. In fact, it might be said that one of the distinguishing marks of the many committed clinical laboratory professionals is their active involvement in the governance process, at the local, state, or federal level.

Knowing government's considerable influence on the profession, laboratory practitioners in leadership positions take responsibility for the appropriateness of the laws and regulations that affect their profession. They participate and encourage their colleagues to participate as private citizens in the process of electing and communicating with lawmakers and other public officials. They also exercise this responsibility by participating and encouraging their colleagues to participate in national associations representing the profession, such as the American Society for Clinical Laboratory Science.

Professional organizations provide mechanisms by which current and pending federal and state legislative and regulatory developments are monitored and assessed. They also are the source of new legislative and regulatory proposals. And they provide a means through which the views of their members can be expressed effectively to lawmakers and other government officials.

In addition to government influences on professional practice, laboratorians have an inherent duty to the patient. The ASCLS Code of Ethics addresses this duty.

History, new scientific and technical developments, competition, laws and regulations, health care cost containment, and ethics are issues vital to the clinical laboratory practitioner. In fact, in the early years of this century we are witnessing clinical laboratory scientists taking a more interactive role with patients and other providers to teach, explain, and advise about laboratory testing. Technology remains very important, but today's laboratory professionals no longer just operate instruments. The field has become more and more collegial with other health care practitioners. Those considering this field should be aware that these are exciting and still evolving times in which to be a clinical laboratory professional.

7

CLINICAL LABORATORY SCIENCE: AN INTERNATIONAL PERSPECTIVE

Canada

Canada has a rich history in preparing professionals to work in its clinical laboratories. Current personnel numbers include 22,000 to 24,000 medical laboratory technologists who are graduates primarily of three-year programs (two years in a community college and a one-year internship). Results of a survey released in the spring of 2000 show a nationwide shortage of medical laboratory technologists. A report published in May 1999 by the Advisory Committee of Health Human Resources predicts that there will be a serious shortage of laboratory personnel within the next five to ten years. According to the report, approximately 16 percent of technologists are expected to retire in five years, and 33 percent plan to retire within the next ten years. Meanwhile, training programs in Canada have been cut back or eliminated in recent years.

According to Kurt Davis, the executive director of the Canadian Society for Medical Laboratory Science: "Based on current enrollment figures, there won't be enough graduates to replace those who will retire over the next ten years." For those with the aptitude for and interest in the health sciences, this is an excellent time to pursue a laboratory technologist career in Canada.

The following represents information on Canadian colleagues as provided by the Canadian Society for Medical Laboratory Science (CSMLS). As you will see, the definition and scope of professional practice is close to that found in the United States. The major difference is that in the United States a baccalaureate degree is required. In Canada the predominant program includes a 2 + 1–year curriculum. However, the CSMLS supports a transition to a baccalaureate education at the entry-to-practice level by the year 2010.

Definition of the Profession in Canada

Medical laboratory technology in Canada is not a single, defined technology; it is a family of technologies that have developed over many years. Starting with traditional areas of histotechnology and bacteriology, areas including hematology, transfusion science, and biochemistry later were added. Cytotechnology started out as a subspecialty of histotechnology. More recently, specialties such as cytogenetics, electron microscopy, immunology, and virology have become recognized components of the profession.

Scope of Responsibilities

Because of its diverse nature, medical laboratory science in Canada cannot be defined in a single package. The scope of practice depends on the type of employing institution (whether a general or specialized laboratory) and on whether the technologist holds general certification or specialty certification. The scope of laboratory practice in Canada is continuously changing, as new techniques are developed and as old techniques are superseded by newer tests and methodologies.

Medical laboratory technologists are an important part of the health care team in Canada because the practice of medicine relies increasingly on the availability of laboratory test data. Technologists are responsible for producing accurate and reliable laboratory results essential to the diagnosis, monitoring, and treatment of disease.

General Skills

Medical laboratory technologists perform a wide variety of investigative and analytical procedures that require both technical and interpretive skills. Education in the basic sciences and in physiology enables technologists to understand the basis for and correlation of test results as well as the ability to identify abnormal results. Knowledge of both theoretical principles and technical skills associated with a broad range of testing procedures ensures that laboratorians are able to keep up with the rapidly changing field of medical laboratory science.

Quality Control

Monitoring the quality of laboratory test results is an important part of the role of laboratory technologists in Canada. They are required to establish, implement, and monitor routine internal quality control programs and to take corrective action if tests are out of control. In many parts of this nation, technologists are also expected to participate in external quality assurance programs.

Laboratory Safety

The clinical laboratory utilizes hazardous reagents. Its personnel also handle infected materials from patients. Medical laboratory technologists have the knowledge and expertise in safely storing, handling, and disposing of hazardous reagents; in the use of laboratory safety equipment; and in the techniques of safe handling and disposal of infectious materials.

Other Services

The role of medical laboratory technologists in Canada also may include:

- assignment and supervision of the work of laboratory support staff
- instruction and supervision of students in the clinical phase of training
- method evaluation and instrument evaluation
- participation in hospital infection control programs
- support of diagnostic services outside of the laboratory, including the patient's bedside

Professional Interactions

Personnel in clinical laboratories produce a wide variety of laboratory test data. This information is essential to the diagnosis of disease and to the treatment and monitoring of the patient. Medical laboratory technologists may function at "arms length" from the physician, with the specimens or requests for laboratory investigation being conveyed through ward clerks or nurses and the laboratory reports through the hospital delivery service.

New diagnostic procedures now make it possible for some of these tests to be requested, conducted, and reported at the patient's bedside, either by the medical technologist or another appropriately trained member of the health care team.

Communication among the laboratory staff, physician groups, nursing staff, and blood collection teams is essential to ensure that the correct specimens are collected at appropriate times. In Canada the responsibility for interpreting laboratory results and advising clinicians (physicians) on appropriate additional tests and/or patient management rests with the laboratory medical staff. It is the responsibility of medical laboratory technologists to call the attention of the laboratory medical staff to abnormal or unusual results. Outside regular working hours and in smaller hospitals that do not have laboratory physicians on staff, technologists interface directly with clinicians.

Other Laboratory Personnel in Canada

In Canada the majority of laboratories employ medical laboratory technologists to perform the laboratory work required in those organizations. There are few technicians in practice in Canada as compared to the United States. (With the pressures of health reform in this nation, such practices are currently under scrutiny.) Lab aides and assistants are used for phlebotomy, sample preparation, clerical, data entry, media preparation, and general cleanup. The private sector tends to use a higher ratio of aides or assistants to support the technologists who are usually operating high volume instruments.

Education and Credentialing

In earlier days the education of medical laboratory technologists in Canada was accomplished through in-service or apprenticeship programs in hospitals. As the complexity of laboratory services increased, it became difficult for individual health care institutions, especially hospitals, to provide the academic and theoretical aspects of training. This led to a transition from hospital-based programs to two-phase programs, in which the didactic education has been provided through an educational institution (usually a community college) with the clinical practice phase completed in a hospital laboratory.

Entrants into medical laboratory technology programs must have senior matriculation (Grade 12), and most programs require science and mathematics as minimum prerequisites.

Other Organizations

Another organization, the Canadian Association of Medical Laboratory Educators (CAMLE) is concerned with the education of practitioners. Membership includes medical laboratory educators in both the didactic and clinical phases of Canadian medical laboratory training programs.

Each province has an organization that represents the profession in that province. In Quebec, l'Ordre professionnel des technologistes médicaux du Québec is the regulatory body established under the Professional Code of Quebec to regulate professional practice. In New Brunswick, Alberta, and Saskatchewan, the provincial society serves as both the regulatory body and the professional society. The College of Medical Laboratory Technologists of

Ontario is the regulatory body; the provincial society is a separate organization.

Accreditation. Accreditation of educational programs is carried out by the Conjoint Committee on Accreditation of Educational Programs for Medical Laboratory Technologists. This committee is sponsored by the Canadian Medical Association and includes representation from other professional organizations, including the Canadian Society for Medical Laboratory Science.

Each accredited program is re-evaluated every five years through application, submission of relevant documentation, and an on-site survey. Both the academic and clinical phases of training are accredited.

Currently, there are close to thirty accredited training programs in Canada, although a few of these programs are under review or revision. Health care reform in Canada has reduced numbers of health care institutions and providers. Of the Canadian programs, two currently involve a university degree (the University of Alberta and the University of Windsor/St. Clair). Other colleges are currently moving toward four-year degree programs.

Certification. Formal certification in medical laboratory technology has been available since 1937 through the Canadian Society of Laboratory Technologists, now known as the Canadian Society for Medical Laboratory Science. The CSMLS conducts certification examinations and also publishes syllabi of study. Certification at the advanced level also is offered by the CSMLS for those who wish to enhance their career status through advancing their knowledge, skills, and professional qualifications.

CSMLS is the national certification body as well as the professional society in Canada. With the evolution of other professional regulatory bodies, the CSMLS national certification program is established as the entry-level standard for the profession. This arrangement ensures one standard for the nation and ensures transferability of credentials across the country.

Moreover, CSMLS is the only national society of laboratory professionals in Canada. It represents fourteen thousand of the eighteen thousand or so Canadian medical laboratory technologists. This provides for the unanimity of the profession. Each province has a provincial society that has a close working relationship with the national society, especially in areas such as continuing education and public relations. The CSMLS has a very helpful website (keyword "CSMLS").

In addition to Canada, most other countries in the world have laboratory professionals as an integral part of their health care systems.

The International Association of Medical Laboratory Technologists (IAMLT) has compiled a directory of laboratory science education programs in countries around the world. These programs vary in content, length, curricula, and titles of professionals. A summary of seven European programs follows, excerpted from the *International Directory of Medical Laboratory Science Education*, 1994, with updates from the 2000 edition.

Finland

Medical laboratory study in Finland dates to the early 1950s. At that time the study was offered at the upper secondary level (tenth to twelfth grades). The first technical laboratory assistants graduated in 1954 from a one-year program. By 1963 the training was extended to two years; by 1966 the qualification was upgraded to "medical laboratory technician." In 1971 the training of medical laboratory technicians was extended to two years six months and specialization training was introduced. By 1970 medical laboratory technicians were included in the Law on Health Care Practice.

A new program of training for medical laboratorians was approved by the national Board of Vocational Education and was implemented in 1987. Since that time the title medical laboratory technologist has been used. (Note: titles are given in two languages—Finnish and Swedish—to reflect the bilingual nature of the country's educational system.)

Since 1987 graduates have been called medical laboratory technologists rather than technicians. The majority of applicants are admitted following completion of secondary school and then complete three and one-half years of study to earn the title of Laboratoriohoitaja/Laboratorieskotare, now translated as medical laboratory technologist.

Polytechnics (ammattikorkeakoulu) constitute a new sector in Finnish education. They were established during education reforms of the 1990s and were based on schools that had provided postsecondary vocational education. The polytechnics amalgamated several institutions to create wider offerings and higher standards. The Finnish Parliament adopted permanent legislation in the mid-1990s and began granting licenses to polytechnics. The Higher Education Council evaluates applications for a license based on the performance of the schools. As of August 2000, all polytechnics operate on a permanent basis.

The network of polytechnics covers the entire country. The degree program in Biomedical Laboratory Science/Biomedical Laboratory Technology is given in seven polytechnics. The master, licentiate, and Ph.D. education in health sciences is offered at the university level. Since 1995 the Bachelor of Biomedical Laboratory Science/Biomedical Laboratory Technology program is three and a half years long during which the student earns 140 credits (210 European transfer credits). The average academic year amounts to 40 credits.

Levels and Length of Training

1. Laboratory technologist (Laboratoriohoitaja/Laboratorieskotare) involves a four-year program following nine years of basic schooling. The program consists of a one-year introductory sequence and three years of subject specialization.
2. Secondary high school graduates enter directly the three-year phase of study.
3. Six-months training in administration leads to a position as department head.
4. A four-year program for the first degree in health sciences, Terveydenhuollon kandidaatti/Hälsovårdskandidat, provides an opportunity for studies to the doctoral level.

Scope of the Field

Increasing automation of the field has simplified tasks. The new study program includes increased research opportunities and also increased patient contact. As a result, the program includes a generous amount of study in general education and behavioral and social sciences as well as management subjects.

Medical laboratory technologists work as a part of the health team in central university hospitals, regional hospitals, municipal hospitals, and health centers and in private hospitals and research centers.

In clinical laboratory work, Finnish health care regulations distinguish the following areas of study: clinical chemistry, clinical hematology, clinical microbiology and virology, clinical physiology, isotopes, clinical histology and cytology, and clinical neurophysiology. There is a distinction regarding the need for specialization at the various levels of hospitals. All laboratories, including health care centers, perform the most common tests of clinical chemistry and hematology and to some extent clinical physiology and microbiology. The laboratories in the central hospitals provide all of the specializations.

Professional Recognition

Accreditation. Accreditation is through the National Board of Vocational Education of the Ministry of Education.

Licensure, Certification, and Registration. Medical laboratorians wishing to practice in Finland must apply to the Department of Health for certification in order to be placed on a list of qualified health personnel. Those whose training is recognized as suitable by the Department of Health also may be certified to practice.

Equivalency/Reciprocity. In the Scandinavian countries, Finnish medical laboratorians can relatively easily be employed.

France

Originally, laboratory work in France was confined to specialized nurses or chemists' aides. In 1954 the Ministry of Education introduced the first programs leading to the Brevet de Technicien d'Analyses Biologiques (Technician Certificate in Biological Analysis), which in 1962 became the Brevet de Technicien Supérieur d'Analyses Biologiques (Higher Technician Certificate in Biological Analysis). Since these initial efforts to organize laboratory training, several developments have taken place: the establishment, in 1965, of a Brevet de Technicien en Biologie (Technician Certificate in Biology), which in 1969 was changed to the technical baccalaureate in biochemistry and in biology. In 1967 the Ministry of Health created the Diplôme d'État de Laborantins d'Analyses Médicales (State Diploma of Medical Laboratory Technology), which is now the basic qualification in medical laboratory technology.

There are currently two levels of study in medical laboratory technology:

1. At the technologist (technicien supérieur) level, programs comprise two years of postsecondary education. Presently there are three such programs that lead to the basic qualifications for employment as a medical laboratory technologist:

The Diplôme d'État de Laborantins d'Analyses Médicales (D.E.L.A.M., State Diploma of Medical Laboratory Technology), which is offered in one of the medical laboratory schools (École de Laborantin d'Analyses Médicales (E.L.A.M.).

The Brevet de Technicien Supérieur (B.T.S., Higher Technician Certificate) with specialization in biological analysis or biochemistry, which is offered in lycées.

The technicien supérieur de laboratoire (the higher laboratory technician), which is undertaken in an Institut Universitaire de Technologie leading to a Diplôme Universitaire de Technologie (D.U.T., University Diploma of Technology).

2. At the secondary-school level, the technicien de laboratoire (laboratory technician) is a three-year program leading to the Baccalauréat de Technicien (Technical Secondary School Certificate) in biological sciences with specialization in biochemistry or biology.

As a result of the 1968 law, education for the State Diploma of Medical Laboratory Technology takes place in one of seventeen Écoles de Laborantins d'Analyses Médicales (E.L.A.M.) that usually are affiliated with hospitals. The programs last two years and take place on a full-time basis. The training consists of theoretical classes, practical training, and field work. The E.L.A.M. provides training specifically for medical applications: diagnostic tests and treatment control, prevention of illness, and epidemics.

In contrast the two-year programs in medical laboratory technology for the B.T.S. and D.U.T. give greater emphasis to scientific theory. The subject content and coverage of in pathology and anatomo-pathological techniques is reduced. Both the B.T.S. and D.U.T. diplomas are acceptable for work in medical laboratories and are also appropriate for work in research laboratories, pharmacology, and environmental surveillance with specific options.

Levels and Lengths of Training

1. B.T.S. (Brevet de Technicien Supérieur) in biological analysis or in biochemistry is a two-year full-time postsecondary program given in a lycée;

2. D.U.T. (Diplôme Universitaire de Technologie) in applied biology requires two years of postsecondary study in a university institute of technology and leads to a position as a laboratory technician.

3. D.E.L.A.M. (Diplôme d'État de Laborantins d'Analyses Médicales) leading to a position as a medical laboratory technologist requires two years of full-time postsecondary study in one of the E.L.A.M.s.

Scope of the Field

Training in medical laboratory science in France, at the level of laborantin (medical laboratory technologist), includes the following general areas.

- hematology/immunohematology
- immunology
- microbiology (bacteriology-parasitology-mycology-virology)
- clinical chemistry/physiology
- pathology/cytology/histology
- applied computers

Professional Recognition

Accreditation. Medical laboratory science programs are under the control of the French Ministry of Health.

Licensure. There have been efforts by the ministries of work and of health and the professional unions to create greater uniformity at the beginning of the career as a laboratory technologist (D.E.L.A.M./B.T.S./ D.U.T.).

Germany

Pathology's early roots are in Germany. It is therefore not surprising that the first organized training courses in Germany for technical assistants in medicine started as early as 1896 at the Lette-haus, a school for women in Berlin. By 1912 a formal program and a state examination were established by the Letteverein, an association of former students of the school. The profession was legally established with state controlled training and diplomas in 1921. By that time specialization had already begun to take form. For example, a course in bacteriology was introduced at the Robert Koch Institute for Infectious Diseases in Berlin and steps had begun toward special education in clinical chemistry.

The next version of the program in Germany was a federal law, uniform for all of Germany after 1940 and with legal protection of the title. After that, several education laws changed. In January 1994 the latest education law came into force. Laboratory training now consists of three years of full-time study at a Berufsfach-schule (vocational school) following a minimum of ten years of primary/secondary schooling. Laboratory training is thus at the "higher secondary" level. However, approximately 75 percent of applicants have the Abitur, which qualifies them for university entrance after thirteen years' schooling.

Students who complete the program take a final state examination that is administered by the school. Successful completion of this examination allows the graduates to use the title "Medizinisch-technische Laboratorium Assistent/in (MTLA)" or Medical Technical Laboratory Assistant.

Levels and Lengths of Training

At the first level, laboratory training in Germany is for generalists. In addition to including hematology and immunohematology, clinical chemistry, microbiology, histotechnology, and cytotechnology, the program contains a required six weeks of nursing practice.

(The nursing practice includes first aid, administrative aspects, as well as patient contact type experiences.)

There are several advanced training programs:

1. Fachassisten/in (specialist) in clinical chemistry; hematology, including immunology; microbacteriology; and histology, including cytology, which requires 600 hours of training (200 hours of which may be practical course work in one of the above specialties). This is offered after a minimum of three years' work experience.
2. Leitende/r Assistent/in (manager) requires 600 hours of management course work (usually on a part-time basis) after a minimum of two years work experience. Prior training as a specialist is desirable. Students study psychology, sociology, law, administration, accident prevention, and medical documentation.

Scope of the Field

The primary level of education for medical laboratorians in Germany is for the generalist. It should be noted that nuclear medical technology is included in the radiological technology training and not in the medical laboratory training.

Professional Recognition

Accreditation. All schools and diplomas for laboratorians are controlled by the German government through the Bundesminister fur Gesundheit (Ministry of Health) under federal law.

Certification. Certificates are granted by State authority after students have passed an examination at the school.

Licensure. Only persons who have passed the State examination administered by the Examination Council of approved schools are licensed and may perform laboratory tests in hematology (including immunology and coagulation), immunohematology, clinical chemistry, microbiology (including bacteriology, parasitology, virology, and serology), and histology (including histopathology and cytology).

Reciprocity

The possibility for medical laboratory technologists educated outside of Germany to work in German laboratories is highly dependent on the availability of work opportunities. The government provides a work permit. German medical laboratory technologists have found recognition of their credentials in other German-speaking countries, such as Austria, Liechtenstein, and Switzerland.

Italy

After completion of high school education (years nine to thirteen), there are two options for education in medical laboratory technology in Italy:

1. The Diploma of Biomedical Laboratory Technologist, offered by universities, which has a duration of three years (2,400 hours of theory and practical training) and leads to the title Tecnico Laboratorio Biomedico (Biomedical Laboratory Technologist);
2. The Certificate of Professional Education Program offered by the Health Department, which has a duration of two years. This program is offered in hospital schools and

leads to the qualification Tecnico Laboratorio Medico (Medical Laboratory Technician).

The Health Reform Act of 1993 declared that the training of laboratory/radiology/physiotherapy is available only at a university level, through a special agreement between the university and the National Health Service.

Scope of the Field

Training is included in biochemistry, clinical chemistry, immunology, hematology and immunohematology, cytopathology, microbiology (including virology, bacteriology, mycology, and parasitology), and toxicology.

The technologist can begin a professional career in various structures of the National Health Service, as well as in scientific and experimental research laboratories and clinical medical laboratories.

Professional Recognition

There is no accreditation or licensure system for medical laboratory technologists in Italy, since there is no national board that controls education in medical technology. The only requirement, at present, for practicing the medical technology profession is the possession of a university diploma (Diploma of Biomedical Laboratory Technologist) or the former Hospital Certificate (Certificate of Professional Education). To qualify for work in public laboratories it is required to pass an oral, written, and practical examination. These are administered by the Ministry of Health.

Equivalency/Reciprocity

Diplomas obtained in European countries are usually considered equivalent. Diplomas obtained in non-European countries must be validated by General Directive in Rome.

Norway

From 1967 to 1985, medical technology education in Norway was two years in length. As of 1985 the title of Norway's medical laboratory technologist changed from Fysiokjemiker or Medisinsk Laboratorie-ingeniør to Bioingeniør. At the same time the curriculum was lengthened to three years. Later, in 1988, a degree in cell biology was implemented.

Scope of the Field

The education of medical laboratory technologists in Norway is structured as a unified program, preparing graduates to work in hospital laboratories, research laboratories, and pharmaceutics, and providing them with basic training in clinical chemistry, hematology, immunohematology, blood serology, microbiology, and pathology.

The program also is designed to give medical laboratory technologists sufficient background such that they can evaluate and exercise quality control, participate in new methods, adjust instruments, and complete simple repairs. In addition the program emphasizes the importance of patient contact and communication.

Accreditation of programs is via the Ministry of Education Research and Church Affairs.

Licensure

On successful completion of the examination for Bioingeniør, graduates are licensed by the Ministry of Health and Social Affairs. The professional association for medical laboratory technologists is the Norwegian Institute of Biomedical Science, a division of the Norwegian Engineer Organization.

Professional Development

Oslo College offers a two-year part-time program that qualifies graduates to take leading positions in laboratories or teaching positions in one of the schools for medical laboratory technologists. Sør-Trøndelag College offers a one-year part-time program in clinical cytology. Those who wish to become laboratory managers may pursue degree programs in administration at one of the regional colleges or at Norges Kommunal og Sosialhøgskole (College of Municipal and Social Studies), Department of Health and Hospital Administration. There also are possibilities of university degrees in biochemistry, cell biology or other subjects relevant to the field of biomedical science.

Equivalency/Reciprocity

The equivalencies of foreign trained medical laboratory technologists are determined by the District Medical Officer of Health in Oslo.

Sweden

Medical laboratory science education in Sweden dates to 1883, when a clinical laboratory was established in Uppsala for clinical diagnostics and practical medicine. Five years later this was followed by a bacteriological laboratory at the Institute of Pathology in Lund. In these early laboratories, the physicians themselves performed laboratory examinations and experiments. Over the years they took on assistants, who learned by experience as no formal programs were available. As late as the 1940s, there was no uniform training in medical laboratory science. Various practical training programs extended from one to three years.

The year 1942 is an important one in the history of medical laboratory technology in Sweden. That year the medical laboratory technologists and the nurses were organized to work toward better and more unified training. Members of the medical laboratory organization then had to have two years of training in a laboratory. In 1945 the first theoretical course in histopathology was held. It covered two years of practical training with theory lessons two nights a week. Subjects of study were: anatomy, histology, chemistry, photography, bacteriology, and pathology; also included were laboratory experiments.

The first official medical laboratory school (Laborantskola) was established in 1957. The thirteen laboratory programs are now college/university-level programs offered in institutions variously referred to as Värdhögskolor (College of Health Caring Sciences) or Hälsohögskolan (University of Health). The basic program for the title of medical laboratory technologist, or laboratorie-assistent, lasts two and one-fourth years (or ninety points). According to the Swedish educational system, each week of study equals one point, and the complete academic year consists of forty points. Graduates of the medical laboratory technology program receive the college or university certificate in medical laboratory technology.

Following educational reform in 1993, all programs now comprise 120 points (three years).

Between 1994 and 2000 the Swedish educational program changed dramatically. In 1999 a new law was enacted. A three-year program of full-time study (120 points) now leads to an examination as a biomedical laboratory scientist, and a B.Sc. in biomedical laboratory science has replaced earlier programs.

Levels and Lengths of Training

Basic biomedical laboratory education
- 120 points
- three years full-time education including twenty weeks laboratory practice
- an examination (thesis) project covering ten weeks of studies

Master's degree
- a minimum of 160 points (includes 120 in basic biomedical laboratory education)
- a major subject of at least 80 points
- a degree project (thesis) of 20 points

Licentiate degree
- 80 points
- corresponds to 50 percent of the studies toward a doctorate degree

Doctoral degree
- requires four years full-time studies or eight years part-time following the first degree

Scope of the Field

Education in medical laboratory science in Sweden prepares the graduate for the profession of medical laboratory technologist in laboratories for health and medical care, in biomedical and veterinary research, in the pharmaceutical industry, and in related aspects of the food industry. The medical laboratory technologist is responsible for the technical procedures of analysis and for the routine working of common types of laboratory instruments and quality control. Other functions include medical tests and research work in which patient contact is an important element.

Education for medical laboratorians is divided into five specializations or tracks:

- clinical chemistry (including hematology and blood banking)
- microbiology
- morphological cell biology (previously histopathology)
- clinical physiology
- biochemistry/molecular biology

Professional Recognition

Accreditation. The Värdhögskolor (Colleges of Health and Caring Sciences) are government institutions. The National Board of Universities or Universitets-högskole ämbelet (UHÄ) sets general and specific goals and specifies the main program content.

Licensure. There is no legal requirement for practice in Sweden.

Certification. Professional recognition is graduation from the medical laboratory specialization (laboratorie-assistentlinjen) in a health care program at a Health Care College (Värdhögskola). The certificate is Högskoleexamin i biomedicinsk laboratorievetenskap, or University Certificate in Biomedical Laboratory Science.

Equivalency/Reciprocity

The equivalencies of foreign trained medical laboratory technologists are determined by the National Board of Health. The board is the designated competent authority under European Community directives on mutual recognition of diplomas concerning the health professions.

United Kingdom

Three grades of staff are employed in the U.K. National Health Service pathology laboratories. These are medical laboratory scientific officers (MLSOs), clinical scientists, mainly biochemists, and medical laboratory assistants (MLAs).

The largest number of personnel in hospital laboratories are employed at various levels of the medical laboratory scientific officer grade, the U.K. equivalent of medical technologists. Appropriately qualified MLSOs may transfer to the scientist grade. Clinical scientists have scientific degrees and higher degrees. Their work is mainly concerned with research and development and the investigation of patients with unusual diagnostic or therapeutic problems. They also provide advice to clinicians on the appropriateness of diagnostic investigations and their interpretations.

There is no qualifying system for medical laboratory assistants. Participants undergo only on-the-job training and undertake a limited range of duties under supervision.

A post-basic qualification examination, leading to the Fellowship of the Institute of Medical Laboratory Sciences (FIMLS), was introduced in 1966, again with no formal courses. In 1977 this examination was substantially altered and two-year courses became mandatory. This examination was further altered in 1987. The first specialized degree in medical laboratory sciences commenced in 1976 at the University of Portsmouth.

Levels and Length of Training

Bachelor's Degrees. Almost half of those entering the trainee level of medical laboratory scientific officers are graduates with bachelor's degrees, 11 percent of whom have specialist degrees in biomedical sciences. It seems likely that the occupation will become bachelor's-level graduate-only entry as is the case in Scotland and Northern Ireland. Most life sciences are acceptable for entry, as are many degrees in chemistry, biochemistry, and microbiology. Entrants with these qualifications are required to follow a two-year, on-the-job training program before their oral examination for state registration.

BTEC Higher National Certificate/Diploma. Almost another half of the entries to the profession in hospitals are recruited with two majors, usually in chemistry or biology, although other science subjects also are acceptable. These students are employed as trainee medical laboratory scientific officers. These students follow a two-year, part-time course of day-release studies at a college leading to the BTEC Higher National Certificate (HNC) in Science, concurrently a three-year, on-the-job training program.

Specialist Bachelor's Degrees in Biomedical Sciences. The first specialist degree in medical laboratory sciences, known as biomedical sciences in the United Kingdom, was introduced in 1976. Since that time more than a dozen such degrees have been established. These degrees are independently generated, and their academic content has been validated by the university offering them.

Master of Science Degree (M.Sc.). There are a number of master's-level or M.Sc. degrees in biomedical sciences and cognate subjects. A number of these courses have been accredited by the IMLS, and successful candidates then may be awarded FIMLS.

Scope of the Field

The majority of the medical laboratory scientific officers are employed in the National Health Service. Thus, the largest single group of medical laboratory scientific officers (MLSOs) are those working in hospital pathology laboratories. However, some MLSOs work in medical schools, pharmaceutical and industrial establishments, and veterinary and public health laboratories. Other MLSOs are in the field of private medicine, and a small number are lecturers in the medical laboratory science specializations.

Professional Recognition

Validation. National certificates and diplomas and higher national certificates and diplomas are validated by the Business and Technician Education Council. Degrees are validated by the university.

Accreditation. Bachelor's and master's degrees are accredited for professional purposes by the Institute of Biomedical Sciences.

Certification. To practice as an MLSO in the National Health Service, personnel must be state-registered by the Council of Professions Supplementary to Medicine.

Equivalency/Reciprocity

For foreign-trained laboratorians, reciprocity is decided on an individual basis and foreign-trained laboratorians who wish to practice in the United Kingdom have to present their credentials and experience to the Council for Professions Supplementary to Medicine for registration, and to the Institute of Biomedical Sciences for professional purposes.

8

Opportunities in the
Armed Services

THERE ARE THREE branches of the armed forces that include laboratory personnel: the air force, army, and navy. Each of the three services is outlined below. In addition to the educational opportunities offered by each, all three services share the eighteen-month Specialist in Blood Banking program (SBB). This program is taught at Walter Reed Army Medical Center in Washington, D.C., and results in a master's degree and certification as a specialist in blood banking. There is also a tri-service professional society, the Society of Armed Forces Medical Laboratory Scientists, which hosts annual meetings and provides opportunities for continuing education to the U.S. Army, Air Force, and Navy.

Opportunities for United States Air Force Biomedical Laboratory Officers

Biomedical laboratory officers in the air force manage, supervise, and perform analyses of biologic and related materials in hospital, environmental/occupational, epidemiological, toxicology, or research and development laboratories. They also teach in medical/clinical laboratory sciences.

Generally, a biomedical laboratory officer manages a medical laboratory or one or more areas of a laboratory located in an air force clinic, small hospital, regional hospital, or medical center. Some officers are assigned to reference laboratories that specialize in performing environmental/occupational, epidemiological, and toxicological analyses. Others are assigned to organizations that are involved in medical research and development. In each instance they are responsible for the accuracy, precision, and validity of all procedures. Responsibilities include the development of new procedures, staying current in regulatory requirements and scientific developments, and updating the laboratory with state-of-the-art equipment.

Laboratory officers maintain active communications among physicians, nurses, administrators, and other officers to provide effective patient care and to enhance the capability of the medical service to support its various missions. Formal and informal continued training of medical laboratory specialists (enlisted personnel) is also expected of laboratory officers.

In 2001 there were 226 biomedical laboratory officers in the United States Air Force.

Wartime Role

Officers will be given increased responsibilities in procuring, collecting, storing, and transporting blood and blood products at the Armed Services Whole Blood Processing Laboratory, contingency blood donor centers, and Transportable Blood Transshipment Centers, and as theater blood program managers and medical treatment facilities managers. The majority of laboratory officers will be mobilized and assigned to manage laboratories in the Expeditionary Medical Support Systems plus 10 (EMED+10), and larger, up to and including the Air Force Theater Hospital. In addition some laboratory officers will operate the biological augmentation teams that have the capability to rapidly isolate and identify biological agents of mass effect. Other laboratory officers will be assigned to each of the hospitals projected as continental United States combat casualty treatment centers.

Selection and Specialty Qualifications

Certification/Registration

Those officers working as general laboratory officers are expected to be registered medical technologists with the Board of Registry of the American Society of Clinical Pathologists (ASCP), the National Credentialing Agency for Laboratory Personnel (NCA), or an equivalent certifying agency acceptable to the Air Force Surgeon General. Officers with subspecialties (advanced degree officers) are expected to seek professional recognition from civilian national certifying boards or agencies such as the American Society for Microbiology,

American Association of Clinical Chemists, or subspecialty certification through the proper medical laboratory certifying agency.

Experience

A minimum of twenty-four months of experience is mandatory in biomedical laboratory assignments and is required for designation as a fully qualified biomedical laboratory officer.

Pay/Rank

Entry-level pay grade is based on a formula offering credit for advanced degree, certification, and work experience. For example, a new officer who possesses a baccalaureate degree and certification but without work experience would enter the service as a second lieutenant. A new officer with a doctoral degree and no certification or work experience may enter the service as a captain. In addition to salary, health care professionals receive tax-free food and housing allowances, as well as bonuses for signing on with the air force. Benefit packages are generous, and include thirty-day paid leave each year.

Career Advancement and Enhancement

Several avenues for career advancement and enhancement are available to the biomedical laboratory officer.

1. Continuing medical education (CME). Officers are expected to have twenty hours of CME each year. Some CME is available to laboratory officers at their assigned medical treatment facilities. Professional laboratory societies on the local, state, and national levels provide

meetings periodically for continuing medical education. Usually the laboratory officer is funded by the hospital once per year for national society meetings. Laboratory officers who present scientific papers or posters are usually funded each year to attend the annual meeting of the Society of Armed Forces Medical Laboratory Scientists, at which the opportunity exists to obtain additional continuing education.

2. Tuition assistance for attendance to off-duty education courses (attendance at night classes in pursuit of a Master of Business Administration). These courses are often provided on-base as extension courses through local universities.

3. Air Force Institute of Technology Graduate Education Programs. Based on air force requirements, laboratory officers are selected to attend various civilian institutions for graduate education.

4. Officers are selected annually for fellowships in blood banking, quality assurance, advanced laboratory management, and medical readiness. (The number selected is based on the requirements of the air force.)

5. Formal professional military education (PME) courses prepare officers for advancement within the military. In addition PME prepares officers who desire to branch out of the laboratory to enter positions commonly held by administrative personnel in civilian health care facilities.

6. Opportunities for advancement in laboratory management, laboratory education, and specialties (including research) can all be incorporated into the biomedical laboratory officer's career program.

United States Air Force Medical Laboratory Specialists (Enlisted Personnel)

Air force enlisted laboratory technicians (equivalent to medical laboratory technicians) complete a fifty-three-week course in the laboratory sciences. The title of the course is Medical Laboratory Specialist. It is divided into two segments referred to as phase I and phase II. Provisions are available for proficiency advancement through these courses.

The medical laboratory specialist (phase I) course is seventeen weeks in length. This course is located at the School of Health Care Sciences, Sheppard AFB, Texas. The course encompasses basic theory and skills, collection, preparation, and analysis of biological fluids and other substances by standard procedures used in medical laboratories to aid in the diagnosis, treatment, and prevention of disease. The emphasis is on routine methodologies employed in the fields of urinalysis, hematology, blood banking, immunology, clinical chemistry, bacteriology, mycology, parasitology, medical laboratory automated data processing, and workload reporting. Three days of this course are designated for "basic medical readiness."

The medical laboratory specialist (phase II) course is a thirty-six-week course. This course is laboratory-based at several air force medical facilities. Its emphasis is on the fundamental techniques used in a medical laboratory. Students develop an understanding of routine laboratory procedures and are trained to perform basic laboratory tests with a minimum of supervision. In addition they gain a knowledge of medical subjects to the extent necessary for their effective performance as medical laboratory specialists.

The mode of instruction for these courses is formal lectures and laboratory (performance) experience.

Educational opportunities available to enlisted members of the air force include, but are not limited to, the following:

- Community College of the Air Force. This community college offers an associate degree for many of the air force specialties.
- Tuition assistance. Assistance is provided to offset the cost of attending off-duty education courses in pursuit of college-level degrees.
- GI Bill. This is provided to offset the cost of college education.
- Professional military education. This is provided to enhance both personnel retention and advancement.
- Eligibility to apply for commissioning as an Air Force Biomedical Laboratory Officer with a bachelor's degree and appropriate laboratory science certification.

Currently there are approximately 1,200 enlisted laboratory personnel assigned to this career field. The number of enlisted in training is dependent on the number of projected vacancies. During 2001 there were 180 entries into these training programs.

Opportunities for United States Army Clinical Laboratory Officers

Commissioned clinical laboratory officers in the U.S. Army manage hospital and clinic laboratories in fixed and field medical treatment facilities in both peacetime and during war. They provide blood, logistical services, and scientific analysis of biologic and related materials in hospital or research laboratories. They also teach in the medical and clinical laboratory sciences.

Generally, an entry-level clinical laboratory officer (clinical laboratory scientist or medical technologist) does not work as a staff technologist, as is the case for many nonmilitary medical technologists. Entry-level duties start at the basic supervisor/manager level. Depending upon the size and complexity of the laboratory to which assigned, the army laboratory officer may function as a section supervisor in a large medical center, as an assistant laboratory manager in a medium-sized community hospital, as a laboratory manager in a small clinic, or as a platoon leader in a medical logistics battalion responsible for collection, storage, and processing of blood.

Clinical laboratory officers are responsible for the overall management of laboratories and for the quality of service, accuracy, precision, and validity of all laboratory test services. Responsibilities also include the development of new procedures, updating the laboratory with state-of-the-art equipment, and staying current and implementing regulatory requirements from such agencies as: the Joint Commission on Accreditation of Healthcare Organizations (JCAHO), the College of American Pathologists (CAP), the Food and Drug Administration (FDA), the American Association of Blood Banks (AABB), the Occupational Safety and Health Administration (OSHA), the Department of Transportation (DOT), Office of Clinical Laboratory Affairs (OCLA), and the Clinical Laboratory Improvement Amendments of 1988 (CLIA) as implemented by the corresponding Department of Defense program (Clinical Laboratory Improvement Program).

Laboratory officers must maintain active communications among pathologists and relevant physicians, nurses, administrators, and other officers to provide accurate, effective, quality patient care and to enhance the capability of the medical service to support its various missions. Formal and informal continued training of medical laboratory specialists (enlisted personnel), medical laboratory technician trainees (civilian personnel), and clinical laboratory scientists/medical technologists also is expected of army clinical laboratory officers. In 2001 there were 112 clinical laboratory officers on active duty around the world with the U.S. Army. An additional 48 officer positions were authorized in the U.S. Army Reserve.

Wartime Role

Clinical laboratory officers have increased responsibilities during wartime. The majority of laboratory officers are mobilized (temporarily sent to a wartime location) and assigned to manage combat support hospital laboratories or general hospital laboratories in the combat zone or in hospital laboratories at selected overseas or U.S. sites scheduled to receive casualties. Additional officers are mobilized to support laboratory epidemiology efforts and to support the increased responsibilities for the procurement, collection, storage, transport, and delivery of blood and blood products to worldwide medical attention facilities for our use in the treatment of soldiers, sailors, and air personnel.

Selection and Specialty Qualifications

Certification/Registration

Officers selected as clinical laboratory officers are required to be registered medical technologists with the Board of Registry of the American Society of Clinical Pathologists (ASCP), or as clinical laboratory scientists with the National Credentialing Agency for Laboratory Personnel (NCA) or an equivalent certifying agency.

Selection of Laboratory Officers

Approximately four to six new clinical laboratory officers are brought into the active army yearly. A variety of programs supply the active army's needs. Accessioning programs include, the army's medical technology school (Clinical Laboratory Officer Course) at Walter Reed Army Medical Center where outstanding Medical Service Corps officers already in the army are given an opportunity to become registered medical technologists and clinical laboratory officers. In addition there are accessioning programs through the Reserve Officer's Training Corps (ROTC) with educational delays, or direct commissioning of outstanding individuals into the active force. Other programs exist for recruiting clinical chemists, physiologists, and microbiologists.

Personnel interested in becoming clinical laboratory officers, either in the U.S. Army Reserve or on active duty with the U.S. Army, should contact their nearest Army Medical Department Recruiter, the ROTC department at many civilian education institutions, or the U.S. Army Recruiting Command, ATTN: RCHS-MS, 1307 Third Avenue, Fort Knox, KY 40121-2726.

Pay/Rank

Entry-level pay grade is based on a formula offering credit for advanced degrees, certification, and potentially, work experience. For example, a new officer who possesses a baccalaureate degree and certification, would enter service in the army as a second lieutenant. A new officer with a master's degree may enter as a first lieutenant, while an officer with an acceptable doctorate may enter the service as a captain.

In 2001 the starting pay for a second lieutenant ranged from $28,900 to $30,600. Promotion to first lieutenant requires eighteen months (pay range from $37,300 to $38,900). At the rank of captain (four years time-in-service), an officer's pay ranged from $49,200 to $50,600 in 2001. In addition to pay officers enjoy benefits such as a fully paid retirement system, nontaxable income for food and housing allowances, economical term-life insurance, free medical and dental care, economical child care and dependent youth programs, shopping privileges at commissaries and exchanges, and worldwide free travel benefits on a space-available basis.

The salary rates for army clinical laboratory officers are competitive with their civilian counterparts. The higher levels of compensation in the military reflects the increased levels of responsibility at an earlier age, the leadership requirements of the armed forces, and the stresses of military life (including worldwide deployability, long hours without overtime, frequent family moves and potential separations, and the possibility of danger when deployed to an unfriendly country or combat zone).

Career Enhancement

In addition to the advanced civilian and military schooling already discussed, other avenues for career enhancement are available to clinical laboratory officers. These include, but are not limited to, the following:

1. Training for enhancement of military skills. Opportunities include airborne training, air assault training, combat casualty care training, and training for the prestigious expert field medical badge.
2. Continuing medical education (CME). Army officers are expected to document category I, or equivalent, CME yearly. Some CME is available to laboratory officers at

their assigned medical treatment facility. Professional laboratory societies on the local, state, and national levels provide meetings for continuing education. Usually each clinical laboratory officer is funded for attendance and registration fees for attending at least one national meeting per year.

3. Membership in the Society of Armed Forces Medical Laboratory Scientists is afforded to clinical laboratory officers. Most officers who present scientific papers or posters at the meeting are centrally funded for attendance each year. The society gives military officers of all branches a professional organization for attainment of professional skills as a medical laboratorian.

4. Tuition assistance is provided for attendance at off-duty educational courses, such as night or weekend classes for a Master's in Business Administration degree. These courses are often provided "on post" as extension courses through local universities. In most cases, out-of-state tuition charges are normally waived for members of the military.

5. Formal professional military education, such as the Combined Arms Staff School, the Command and General Staff College, and the Army Management College for attainment of executive skills, are available to career officers in the army.

6. Advancement in laboratory management, laboratory education, and a variety of laboratory specialties (including research) can all be incorporated into the clinical laboratory officer's career program. Fellowships and grants may be accepted, and a Training-with-Industry program allows officers to experience firsthand skills required.

United States Army Medical Laboratory Specialists and Sergeants (Enlisted Personnel)

Army enlisted medical laboratory specialists and medical laboratory sergeants (equivalent to medical laboratory technicians), complete a fifty-two week course in laboratory sciences, after attending army basic training and basic combat medical training. The course, Medical Laboratory Specialist (MOS 91K), is divided into two segments.

Phase I of the medical laboratory technician course is taught at the Academy of Health Sciences in the Army Medical Department Center and School at Fort Sam Houston, Texas. This twenty-six-week phase, located in the Department of Clinical Support Services in San Antonio, Texas, encompasses basic laboratory theory and skills, collection, preparation, and analysis of biological fluids and other substances by standard medical laboratory procedures. The emphasis is on routine methods employed in peacetime and wartime hospital laboratories performing tests in urinalysis, hematology, blood banking, immunology, clinical chemistry, bacteriology, and automated data processing.

Phase II of the medical laboratory technician course is a twenty-six-week hands-on clinical rotation that is laboratory-based at several army medical treatment facilities throughout the United States, including Hawaii. Its emphasis is on the fundamental techniques used in a medical laboratory. Students develop proficiency in performance of routine laboratory procedures and are trained to perform moderate and high complexity laboratory tests with a minimum of supervision.

Currently there are approximately two thousand enlisted laboratory personnel assigned to units in the army active component.

Additionally there are more than fifteen hundred opportunities in the U.S. Army Reserve for assignment of medical laboratory technicians or medical laboratory sergeants. The number of enlisted students in training is dependent on projected vacancies. In 2001 approximately 560 students were scheduled to attend medical laboratory technician courses.

Educational Opportunities

Educational opportunities available to enlisted members of the U.S. Army include, but are not limited to, the following:

1. Through the Army Council on Education (ACE), credit for military courses may be accepted toward degree requirements of civilian educational institutions. Methods are available for graduates of the medical laboratory specialist course to obtain an applicable associate degree.
2. Tuition assistance is provided to offset the cost of attending off-duty education courses in pursuit of college-level degrees.
3. The GI Bill is also provided to offset the cost of a college education. Its benefits can be used while a service member is in the service, or after completion of enlistment and release from active duty.
4. Professional military education courses and correspondence courses are provided to enhance readiness, personnel growth, retention, advancement, and professional technical skills.

Pay/Rank and Career Advancement

Following the medical laboratory technician course, graduates are assigned to a variety of units, such as: hospital laboratories, field medical units, medical logistics battalions, or research laboratories. At this point soldiers are normally classified as specialist (grade E4) with an annual salary of approximately $21,000 (2001).

After three to five years, the successful laboratory specialist returns to the Academy of Health Sciences for attendance at the Basic Noncommissioned Officers (NCO) Course for Medical Laboratory Sergeants. This fifteen- to seventeen-week course qualifies NCOs to become laboratory supervisors working for laboratory managers or pathologist laboratory directors. These laboratory NCOs provide support in such laboratory areas as personnel management and time scheduling, supply procurement, budgeting, and other daily laboratory operations. Job opportunities include hospital, reference, or research laboratories; various administrative staff positions; blood platoon leadership positions; and instructorships at the Academy of Health Sciences. Additionally, outstanding enlisted medical specialists may apply to attend the one-year cytotechnology course.

Enlisted specialists may advance in rank from private (E1) in basic training to the rank of sergeant major (E9) to cap an enlisted career. College graduates at the associate level, who are certified medical laboratory technicians, may also enter the enlisted laboratory field at the grade of E4 with accelerated promotion to E5 (2001 annual pay, $23,000). These graduates proceed directly to duty assignments as qualified medical laboratory specialists. Significant pay bonuses are available upon reenlistment. At the grade of E8, master sergeants earned approximately $43,600 per year in 2001, in addition to the nonpay benefits previously described for commissioned officers.

For baccalaureate-prepared graduates in biology or chemistry, direct accessions to serve as biological science assistants at the entry grade of E5 are available yearly. These assistants work in Ph.D. directed laboratories in the Medical Research and Material Command to provide research in a variety of soldier related tasks and requirements, including infectious disease research, biological or chemical warfare research, environmental medical research, rapid test kit development, malaria research, physiological research, and vaccine research.

In summary, the U.S. Army has opportunities for clinical laboratory practitioners among its officers and enlisted personnel. In addition, considerable mobility exists in the army for those interested in a career in laboratory science.

United States Navy Officer Program for Medical Technologists

Qualified medical technologists (clinical laboratory scientists) are selected to serve as commissioned officers in the United States Navy. As a commissioned officer, these technologists serve as leaders, managers, and supervisors in state-of-the-art clinical laboratories throughout the United States and in many foreign countries. Contingency or mobilization roles are as integral members of the health care team aboard hospital ships, other navy combatant ships, or service with one of the deployed field hospitals. Additional assignments are as educators in military laboratory schools, as headquarters staff members, or as investigators in medical research facilities.

Selected applicants are normally commissioned as ensigns in the Medical Service Corps. This process is highly selective, and a successful applicant must meet the following criteria:

- baccalaureate degree from an accredited college or university
- certification of a one-year course of study in medical technology by a school or program accredited by the National Accrediting Agency for Clinical Laboratory Science (The NAACLS program completion requirement may be waived if the applicant has at least four years of documented laboratory training or experience.)
- two years of experience in a clinical laboratory
- successful completion of a national medical technology certification examination (Board of Registry of the American Society of Clinical Pathologists or the National Credentialing Agency)
- blood bank experience (considered a plus but not required)

Successful officers are those who can meet the demanding dual responsibilities of a naval officer and clinical professional. Navy laboratory officers are not "bench technologists" but fill challenging roles as laboratory managers, supervisors for other officers, navy enlisted technicians, and civilian laboratory personnel as well as provide professional consultation to the medical staff.

Opportunities and Benefits of the Navy Officer Program

Navy medical technologists are a select group of about ninety officers who provide dynamic leadership in navy clinical laboratories. As commissioned officers, these technologists are continually challenged by increasing responsibilities and have the opportunity to take on these added responsibilities much earlier in their career than their civilian counterparts. They also enjoy increased status and have a chance to work in hospitals throughout the United States and in many foreign countries.

New duty assignments are normally received every three to five years. Significant assignment variety exists as these officers are trained and ready to deploy in support of the American fighting forces. Educational opportunities also abound. These opportunities range from attendance at national professional meetings to full-time graduate education at the master's level for select officers, as well as funded and professional development leadership courses.

Annual salaries (2001 figures) began at $31,000 for a newly commissioned ensign (with more for a married officer and if located in high cost of living areas). After at least four years and two promotions, a navy lieutenant medical technologist earns between $51,000 and $57,500 a year. A navy commander having served twenty years earns approximately $82,000 annually, and a captain with twenty-six years of service earns more than $100,000. A portion of the salary is nontaxable. Career officers are eligible for retirement upon completion of their navy career. A medical technologist retiring from the navy after twenty years service earns 50 percent of base pay. The amount increases with each additional year of active duty, peaking at 75 percent after thirty years of service. A navy captain retiring after thirty years receives $65,800 annually.

Additional benefits available to the navy medical technologist and family include free medical and dental care (discounted dental care for dependents), inexpensive life insurance, shopping at military grocery and discount stores, economical child care, on-base housing in selected locations, and free overseas air travel on a space-available basis.

Further information on a career as a navy medical technologist may be obtained from a local navy recruiter or the navy specialty leader for medical technology.

BIBLIOGRAPHY

Allied Health Education Directory, 1995-1996. 23rd ed. Division of Allied Health Education and Accreditation. Chicago: AMA, 1995.

Allied Health Services; Avoiding Crises: Report of a Study. Division of Health Care Services, Institute of Medicine, National Academy of Sciences. Washington, D.C.: National Academy Press, June 1988.

American Society for Clinical Laboratory Science. *Scope of Practice*. Adopted by the ASCLS House of Delegates, August 2001.

Canadian Society for Medical Laboratory Science, web pages. Hamilton, Ontario, 2001.

Claussen, Frieda. "Meeting of the Board of Registry with Advisory Committee of Medical Technologists, June 1943." *American Journal of Medical Technology*. 9:202-207, 1943.

"Clinical Laboratory Technologists and Technicians." *Occupational Outlook Handbook*, Bureau of Labor Statistics, U.S. Department of Labor, Washington, D.C., U.S. Government Printing Office, 2000–2001 edition.

"Future Directions of Clinical Laboratory Science Education Programs." Position paper. Washington, D.C.: American Society for Medical Technology, June 1987.

Health Professions Career and Education Directory (HPCED), 2001–2002 edition. Chicago: AMA.

Herrick, Vivian. "The Heritage of the Clinical Laboratory." *American Journal of Medical Technology*. 3:53–59, 1937.

Hubbard, Joel D. *A Concise Review of Clinical Laboratory Science*. Williams & Wilkins, 1997.

Ikeda, Kano. "The Present Trends in Medical Technology." *American Journal of Medical Technology*. 17:81–87, 1951.

Karlsson, Britta, Sr. Editor. *International Directory of Medical Laboratory Science Education*. 1994, with updates from the 2000 edition.

Karni, Karen. "Certification for the Profession by the Profession: The Role of NCA." *Clinical Laboratory Science*. 3:243–244, 1990.

Karni, K., K. Viskochil, and P. Amos. *Clinical Laboratory Management: A Guide for Clinical Laboratory Scientists*. Boston: Little Brown and Co., 1982.

Kolmer, John. "The Demand and Training of Laboratory Technicians." *Journal of Laboratory Clinical Medicine*. 3:493–496, 1918.

National Accrediting Agency for Clinical Laboratory Sciences. "Revised Essentials of Accredited Educational Programs for the Clinical Laboratory Scientist/Medical Technologist." Chicago: September 2001.

National Accrediting Agency for Clinical Laboratory Sciences. "List of Accredited Clinical Laboratory Science Programs, 2001." Chicago: January 2001.

Paradis, Adrian. *Opportunities in Military Careers.* Chicago: VGM Career Books, 1999.

Price, Glenda, editor. "The American Society for Medical Technology: A Short History." Houston: American Society for Medical Technology, 1982.

Price, Glenda. "Introduction." *Shaping the Future of Clinical Laboratory Practice: Proceedings of the Conference.* Washington, D.C.: American Society for Medical Technology, 1986.

Rausch, Verna and Karen Karni. "A Tilt at a Windmill? A Study of Medical Technology Education." *American Journal of Medical Technology.* 38:216–228, 1972.

Todd, James C. *A Manual of Clinical Diagnosis.* Philadelphia: W. B. Saunders, 1908.

Vaughan, Victor C. *A Doctor's Memories.* Indianapolis: Bobbs Merrill, 1926.

White, Lavinia. "Thirty-five Years of Medical Technology." *American Journal of Medical Technology.* 31:295–299, 1965.

White, William D. *Public Health and Private Gain: The Economics of Licensing Clinical Laboratory Personnel.* Chicago: Maaroufa Press, Inc., 1979.

Williams, M. Ruth. *An Introduction to the Profession of Medical Technology.* Philadelphia: Lea & Febiger, 1971.

Agencies and Organizations

Accrediting Organizations for Laboratory Education Programs

Accrediting Bureau of Health
Education Schools (ABHES)
803 West Broad Street, #730
Falls Church, VA 22046

National Accrediting Agency for
  Clinical Laboratory Sciences
  (NAACLS)
8410 West Bryn Mawr, Suite 670
Chicago, IL 60631

Certifying Agencies for Graduates of Laboratory Education Generalist Programs

AAB Board of Registry
917 Locust Street, Suite 1100
St. Louis, MO 63101-1413

American Medical Technologists (AMT)
710 Higgins Road
Park Ridge, IL 60068-5765

Board of Registry of American Society of Clinical Pathologists
(ASCP)
2100 West Harrison Street
Chicago, IL 60612

National Credentialing Agency for Laboratory Personnel (NCA)
P.O. Box 15945-289
Lenexa, KS 66285

Professional Organizations of Interest for Laboratory Personnel

American Association of Bioanalysts (AAB)
818 Olive Street, Suite 918
St. Louis, MO 63101

American Association of Blood Banks (AABB)
8101 Glenbrook Road
Bethesda, MD 20814-2749

American Association for Clinical
   Chemistry (AACC)
2101 L Street NW, Suite 202
Washington, D.C. 20037

American Association of Immunologists (AAI)
9650 Rockville Pike
Bethesda, MD 20814

American Association of Pathologists' Assistants
8030 Old Cedar Avenue, #225
Bloomington, MN 55425-1215

American Hospital Association (AHA)
One North Franklin
Chicago, IL 60606

American Medical Electroencephalographic Association
850 Elm Grove Road
Elm Grove, WI 53122

American Society for Clinical Laboratory Science
7910 Woodmont Avenue, Suite 530
Bethesda, MD 20814

American Society of Clinical Pathologists (ASCP)
2100 West Harrison Street
Chicago, IL 60612-3798

American Society of Cytopathology (ASC)
400 West Ninth Street, Suite 201
Wilmington, DE 19801

American Society of Hematology
1200 Nineteenth Street NW, Suite 300
Washington, D.C. 20036-2412

American Society for Microbiology (ASM)
1325 Massachusetts Avenue NW
Washington, D.C. 20005-4171

Association of Genetic Technologists, Inc.
P.O. Box 15945-288
Lenexa, KS 66285

Association of Schools of Allied Health Professions
1730 M Street, Suite 500
Washington, D.C. 20036

Canadian Society for Medical Laboratory Science (CSMLS)
PO/CP 2830, LCD 1/PDF 1
Hamilton, Ontario L8N 3N8

Clinical Laboratory Management Association (CLMA)
9 Old Lincoln Highway, Suite 201
Malvern, PA 19355-2135

National Society for Histotechnology (NSH)
4201 Northview Drive, Suite 502
Bowie, MD 20716-2604

Society of Nuclear Medicine (SNM)
1850 Samuel Morse Drive
Reston, VA 22090-5316

About the Author

Karen Karni, Ph.D., is former Professor and Director of the Division of Medical Technology (Clinical Laboratory Science), University of Minnesota Medical School. She has authored more than sixty articles and chapters in education and management in laboratory science.

Dr. Karni has been active in the American Society for Clinical Laboratory Science (ASCLS) for more than thirty years and has received numerous awards from this association: the Sherwood Professional Achievement Award in Education, Immunology Scientific Assembly Award, Scientific Creativity Award, Kleiner Award for excellence in writing in the *American Journal of Medical Technology*, national Member of the Year, and the Mendelson Award for significant and sustaining contributions to the profession. She is a former president of the National Credentialing Agency for Laboratory Personnel and was the 1997–1999 President of ASCLS.

Karen Karni worked as a short-term consultant for Project HOPE in Panama; she also evaluated the medical laboratory technology program at Kuwait University. She has presented papers at the International Association of Medical Laboratory Technologists World Congresses, held in Dublin, Ireland, and in Hong Kong.

Dr. Karni received her B.S. degree in medical technology "with distinction" from the University of Minnesota, and an Ed.M. degree from the University of New York at Buffalo. She earned a Ph.D. degree in education from the University of Minnesota.

This edition was revised with the assistance of Luisa Gerasimo, a freelance writer living in Wisconsin.